Ending Emptiness

I am very thankful for men like Tim Hatch. God has given him keen insight into His Word. He has been gifted the unique ability to communicate that insight in a way that others can easily understand and subsequently apply. I am excited that he decided to put his Godly wisdom on paper, and I know many people will be drawn to Jesus as a result.

–**Matthew Slater**, Wide Receiver, All-Pro
Special Teams Player, New England Patriots

The ministry of Pastor Tim Hatch and Waters Church have helped me change my life! They have helped me get closer to Christ and change the way I live and view life. The emptiness I felt has gone away!

–**Kendrick Bourne**, Wide Receiver, New England Patriots

Today's culture and society reflect lives where one strives to have everything, yet one is still left feeling empty. Pastor Tim Hatch, in his book *Ending Emptiness*, provides relevant insight on how the proper perspective grounded in Jesus Christ can change everything from yearning to a life of fulfillment. A must-read!

–**Bishop Sudarshan J. Komanapalli**, Manna International

In coaching, I have three main things I try to do consistently every day. *Conviction* for what I believe in. *Consistency* in what I coach, teach, and correct. *Passion* for developing our players as men and athletes. Pastor Tim does the same thing. He is *convicted* by the Word of *God*, *consistent* in teaching sound doctrine, and *passion-filled* in his approach to preaching and educating his church. He speaks *truth* that you can only get from knowing what the Bible says and knowing how to teach us to learn and apply God's spoken word to our daily lives.

I look forward to Pastor Tim's sermons and podcasts each week. He is truly a Godly man that walks his faith each and every day. Thank you, PT, for who you are and what you do.

–**Joe Kim**, Skill Development Coach, New England Patriots

Ending Emptiness has helped recenter my focus and attention on the one person who can provide me true peace and joy in the midst of a season of "why" in my life. There was a plan and direction my family and I were moving in, and these plans all fell apart. I entered a period of time questioning God and getting frustrated with God, and these frustrations were spilling into my personal family life and work life.

I began reading *Ending Emptiness* during this season of uncertainty, and it opened my eyes more clearly to the reality that I was making an idol out of the "next thing" in life. I was elevating a family move, a job promotion, and a potential ministry opportunity as things that would make my life better and more fulfilling. These are good things, but the disappointment I was experiencing made me realize maybe I was making them "ultimate" things in my life. *Ending Emptiness* helped me to run to Jesus, the one who suffered greatly in His perfect obedience to not His will but His Father's will, and this created eternal peace between God and me. As I began to see God conforming me into the image of Christ, it took a great burden and anxiety off of my shoulders in this season of "why", and I learned again to rest in Him.

–**Joe Koudelka**, Cumberland, RI

Pastor Tim has done it again. His first book, *Move!* spoke to the theme, "We can't stay here." It did so in an action-packed, quick-paced allegory of "why" through the lens of Scripture, his own experiences, and societal context.

He has accomplished exactly the same rhythm, pace, and biblical answers in *Ending Emptiness*. Not only can we not stay here, but we don't want to. The title draws the reader in, but the conviction on each page invigorates you to dig deeper into the text.

Whether you're a teen getting ready to head to high school or an octogenarian looking back on your life, there is much to consider after a worldwide pandemic. Many of us have had time to do so in isolation and have come out asking, "What's it all for?" This book provides the answer to the question and so much more.

–**Shawn Strok**, Wrentham, MA

Pastor Tim's commentary on "why God puts difficult people in our lives" really helped me view this aspect of my life like never before. It's such a great reminder of "And we know that in all things God works for the good of those who love Him who have been called according to his purpose" (Romans 8:28).

I am excited to apply this and see God move!

–**Manish Bhatia**, Attleboro, MA

ENDING EMPTINESS

Discovering the Ancient Wisdom
that Leads to Endless Abundance

TIM HATCH

NASHVILLE

NEW YORK • LONDON • MELBOURNE • VANCOUVER

ENDING EMPTINESS

Discovering the Ancient Wisdom That Leads to Endless Abundance

© 2024 Tim Hatch

Published in New York, New York, by Morgan James Publishing. Morgan James is a trademark of Morgan James, LLC. www.MorganJamesPublishing.com

Proudly distributed by Publishers Group West®

Morgan James BOGO™

A **FREE** ebook edition is available for you or a friend with the purchase of this print book.

CLEARLY SIGN YOUR NAME ABOVE

Instructions to claim your free ebook edition:
1. Visit MorganJamesBOGO.com
2. Sign your name CLEARLY in the space above
3. Complete the form and submit a photo of this entire page
4. You or your friend can download the ebook to your preferred device

ISBN 9781636983493 paperback
ISBN 9781636983509 ebook
Library of Congress Control Number:
2023949433

Interior Design by:
Chris Treccani
www.3dogcreative.net

Morgan James **PUBLISHING**

Builds

with...
Habitat for Humanity®
Peninsula and Greater Williamsburg

Morgan James is a proud partner of Habitat for Humanity Peninsula and Greater Williamsburg. Partners in building since 2006.

Get involved today! Visit: www.morgan-james-publishing.com/giving-back

To the people I've had the privilege of pastoring for the last two decades in New England. Your lives and your spirits have sustained an incredible span of ministry that has both challenged and inspired me. Pastoring has birthed much wrestling with God over His word to make sure what I tell you is what He says and not my own thoughts. This book is the result of many days and nights seeking God's wisdom for the ready recipient in those seats.

TABLE OF CONTENTS

||||||||||||||||||||||||||||||||||||||||||||||||||||||||||||||||||

III

Having It All Is Not *All* That Great

E rnest Hemingway lived an unparalleled life. He became a literary legend, one of the all-time most influential American writers. In the books he authored and the personal adventures he experienced, he exuded the zeitgeist, or spirit, of the twentieth century—its highs and its lows.

Hemingway was born at the end of the 1800s. As a young man, he served in the American Red Cross during World War I and was wounded twice in Italy, earning a medal for bravery in the process. Then, as a civilian and journalist during World War II, Hemingway patrolled the Cuban coast for German U-boats, accompanied the Allied liberation of Western Europe from Normandy to the German border, and even briefly led a group of French resistance fighters.[1]

The famous writer won a Pulitzer Prize in 1953 and a Nobel Prize in 1954. He got to live and work in exotic places like France, Italy, Cuba, and Key West, Florida, which to this day holds an annual celebration in his name—complete with a Hemingway look-alike contest. He was a successful big-game hunter, bull-fighter, and sports fisherman.

But Hemingway also divorced three times and was unfaithful in all four of his marriages.[2] He suffered two (back to back) airplane crashes, depression, and alcoholism, and ultimately committed suicide at home in Idaho.[3]

In his novel *A Farewell to Arms*, Hemingway describes ants swarming frantically on a burning log, seemingly to represent what he perceives as the frenzied, doomed nature of human existence.[4] Coming from a man who lived beyond the norm, seizing the day and living every moment to the fullest, such a pessimistic, even nihilistic, attitude is especially striking. What does it say that a man who seemed to suck the marrow out of life ultimately found no fulfillment in it?

It says we need more than what this world offers. Today, the imagery of the ants on the burning log sums up well the existence of postmodern man in a world where we can experience almost anything and still feel nothing. We have the ability to live Hemingway's life in many respects, either in real life or virtually. The digital age affords us unfathomable opportunity to travel and experience life as never before, without leaving our home. We can drop ourselves on almost any street in the world through Google Maps. We can order food with a few taps of our fingers and have it delivered to our door. We can invest like a Wall Street broker in real-world industries or digital currencies and turn our fortunes around in an instant. With the rise of the Metaverse, a future where we sit in pods experiencing almost anything we can imagine without moving seems to be just around the corner.

In effect, we could, like Hemingway, live the life we've dreamed—minus the risk of enemy mortars and plane crashes. But are we happier?

I wrote this book to identify and alert you to the real virus seeking to kill you. Believe it or not, its not a pandemic, COVID-19 or otherwise. It's emptiness. A recently published report from the CDC finds that 44 percent of high school students say they feel "persistently sad and hopeless."[5] Another report finds that deaths by alcohol rose 25 percent during the 2020 coronavirus pandemic.[6] Those numbers are shocking, to say the least. And most people who will read this book live in the United States, where we are conditioned to believe more money or friends or notoriety will bring more happiness. But this belief, like most earthly promises, is not true.

Research indicates that the richer we become, the less happy we are.[7] A Harris poll from 2017 showed that only 33 percent of Americans who were surveyed expressed being happy.[8] From 2018 to 2020, the U.S. was ranked nineteenth in the world for happiness levels.[9] Add a COVID-19 pandemic to the mix, relentless inflation, political animosity, unceasing wars, and the constant threat of economic upheaval and the situation has only gotten worse. According to *Healthline*,[10] one study has found that depression symptoms were three times higher during the COVID-19 lockdown. Experts say the COVID-19 pandemic caused physical, emotional, and psychological distress, and not just for patients of the virus. An NBC news headline revealed emergency room doctors are begging for help to treat mental illness in children.[11]

Consequently, people are still anxiously searching for whatever relief their souls need to solve an eternal problem that we know humans do not possess in themselves. We've seen the same story play out before our eyes over and over again. Celebrity after celebrity with a carefully crafted life continues to struggle with drugs, alcohol, and depression, with many of these superficially successful people ultimately taking their own lives. To name a few, we've mourned funnyman Robin Williams, celebrity chef to presidents Anthony Bourdain, designer to the world's elite Kate Spade, and very recently as I write this, country music star Naomi Judd. Let's not forget the infamous 27 Club, comprising cultural powerhouses such as musicians Jim Morrison, Janis Joplin, Jimi Hendrix, Amy Winehouse, and Kurt Cobain, whose lives all ended at the height of their careers and before they reached the age of twenty-seven. Sadly, we've seen the emptiness of our cultural leaders trickle across the social spectrum.

At some point, we have to stop repeating the lie that a better life here on earth, experiencing all it offers, will make us happy. Before Anthony Bourdain, Robin Williams, or Ernest Hemingway, there was an ancient king who lived almost there thousand years ago and was afforded the greatest opportunities of his age. His name was Solomon. And like Hemingway, he traveled the world, lived in exotic places, maintained too many lovers to count (the Bible records at least one thousand romantic involvements).

Also like Hemingway, Solomon wrote world-changing books, including Proverbs and Song of Songs. All three of his books found their place in Holy Scripture. The last of Solomon's works was written as his life was winding down. It's one of my favorites: Ecclesiastes.

The theme of Ecclesiastes is the impetus behind the book you're reading now: the understanding that "all is vanity" (with some translations using words like "meaningless" or "futility" in place of "vanity" in Ecclesiastes 1:2). Solomon discovered this from the heights of fame, intelligence, and success as king of Israel during the climax of her power and status in the ancient world. Solomon's third and final book details honest lessons learned the hard way, by a man who had everything yet felt nothing was truly satisfying.

The theme that worldly pursuits are in vain is something our present age refuses to believe could be true.

Solomon also tells us there really is "nothing new under the sun" (Ecclesiastes 1:9). History repeats itself, and humanity continues the quest for more and better without having learned the lessons of Solomon's experience. There is wisdom to be gained when we shed the false promises of our age, dig deeper into real life with God, and open our hearts to what He wants to give us.

Warning: this book is written to give you more than simple, pat answers to life. I'm a pastor who is *very* familiar with Christians' propensity to boil all of life's challenges down to a single verse, usually taken out of context. This is why I love the book Ecclesiastes. If you sit down to read it, you'll soon find out how complicated it can be to unearth the truths it offers. Ecclesiastes is a synopsis of real life, with no simple answers or pithy solutions. It's honest—dreadfully honest. And it's time for Christians to embrace honesty and nuance in a complex world filled with half-truths and lies. Life is far more challenging than we Christians would often like to admit.

So as you read ahead, do not expect Christian slogans like "let go and let God" or "all things work together." I want to spare you simple formulas, because Solomon doesn't offer them in Ecclesiastes. He offers his life "under the sun," apart from God, and then brings us answers to the inherent complications and complexities—through life with God.

Solomon refers to himself as the Qoheleth, which is a term that can be translated as "the Preacher" (Ecclesiastes 1:1). Now, if you know anything about Solomon's life, you'd never call him a preacher. We expect preachers to live exemplary lives, and Solomon definitely does not fit that bill. Again, Ecclesiastes isn't a book of easy answers. We are invited by Solomon to experience the real difficulties of life and to find the real meaning running through all of it.

First, we have to deconstruct the "happiness chase" our postmodern age offers. Then, we have to understand that life encompasses many seasons and countless extremes. We must learn the lessons of navigating difficult relationships, challenging problems, and most importantly, enjoying life in less-than-desirable conditions. Finally, we have to learn to embrace life as it comes *with God*, creating a story that's far bigger than us.

Oh, and we should do this quickly, as none of us realizes how soon our time in this world may end.

Join me on this journey. Embrace this ancient, down-to-earth instruction manual from a man who had been there, done that, and actually left us the answer to "now what?"

Let's begin.

THE ULTIMATE LIE: "IF I GET WHAT I WANT, I'LL FINALLY BE HAPPY"

Solomon was the son of David, another name you should know. He's the guy who beat Goliath, became king of Israel, and took Israel from ignominy to worldwide fame. David was like the original Instagram influencer, the original winner of *The Voice*, or the SEAL team leader who killed Bin Laden: he was the kind of person young people in America might aspire to be. On top of all that, he had God's approval before men and is listed in Scripture as "a man after God's own heart" (Acts 13:22).

After Israel entered into an era of peace like the kingdom had never before experienced, David handed Solomon the keys to the kingdom, along with all the resources he would ever need to rule and reign over the great superpower that was Israel in 800 B.C.[12]

If you want to talk about a guy who was born with a silver spoon in his mouth, that was Solomon. And his reign made the kingdom even more prosperous. Solomon's story is interesting because he didn't just get the kingdom at a very young age; he also received what I like to call a "blank check from God" moment. That is, one day while Solomon was praying and worshiping the Lord, God showed up and said to him, "Ask for whatever you want, and I will give it to you" (1 Kings 3:1–15).

Wouldn't you love a moment like that with God? (And how many of you would ask for a million more wishes?)

Solomon could have asked for anything, but he responded, in essence, "Lord, I'm young and I'm in charge of this great nation of yours. Who can govern it, really? I don't know what I'm doing, so I'm asking you for wisdom."

God was so impressed by Solomon's request, he said, "Because you … have not asked for a long life or wealth or the death of your enemies—I will give you what you asked for! … And I will also give you what you did not ask for—riches and fame! No other king in all the world will be compared to you for the rest of your life!" (1 Kings 33 11–13 NLT).

God lived up to his promise, and Solomon lived the dream life. Everything he could ever ask for was at his fingertips. If he wanted something, all he had to do was reach for it. But in the end, instead of finding happiness, Solomon found only emptiness.

Like with most people, Solomon's life can be divided into three stages: the excitement of youth, the maturity of age, and the lament of life.

When Solomon was young, he was in love with love. He was so enamored by it, he sang about it—but he didn't just sing it. Like his father before him, he wrote his musical compositions down. He too became published by the Holy Spirit, and his lyrics are recorded in Holy Scripture. We call it the Song of Solomon, and to this day it remains one of the most sexually evocative pieces of literature the world has ever seen. This song is so graphic and so sensual, if a performing artist were to take it to the Superbowl half-time show, it would result in a national outrage that would outstrip and overshadow every previous controversial performance.

Then Solomon entered into middle age and had children, and he suddenly realized, "I've got to leave some wisdom behind for these kids!" So he wrote a book called Proverbs, in which he offered up wisdom and advice so his son and heir wouldn't get tripped up in life by temptation, gluttony, promiscuity, corruption, anger, greed, pride, or deceit as he grew into the leader he was born to be.

And finally, Solomon got old. He came to a place his youth and success had helped him ignore. He looked back on his younger years and his mid-life years and asked, "What is it all really about, really?"

Think about it: the man who had the opportunity to do whatever he wanted, to buy whatever he needed, and to take whatever he desired looked back on his life and said, "Having it all is not that great."

This is how we end up with the book of Ecclesiastes. In it, Solomon is trying to tell us something incredibly important. The truth is, there is only One who can end the emptiness that nothing else in life can fill. We need to ask ourselves some specific questions about our expectations in life before we end up in some luxury hotel suite in Paris, France, knowing we have everything life has to offer—and still believing that life isn't worth living.

CHAPTER ONE

||||||||||||||||||||||||||||||||||||||||||||||||||

The Insanity of Life's Vanity

Vanity of vanities, says the Preacher, vanity of vanities! All is vanity.
What does man gain by all the toil at which he toils under the sun?
—ECCLESIASTES 1:2–3 (ESV)

There's a tendency to believe that life is fulfilling when it's filled with certain things. In our youth, we think, *"When I get out on my own, I'll be happy."* Then we do it and find ourselves lonely. So we turn the page and tell ourselves, *"When I get married, I'll be happy."* And perhaps by God's grace we find a spouse who is just as flawed as we are, and the idyllic romance we assumed would be ours is just two flawed people working out their idiosyncrasies through trials and troubles. It is then we might think, *"Let's have kids—that will make us happy!"* Then, once again by God's grace, we may have kids, and the bills and the responsibilities and the challenges of our parenting pile up.

And then we discover that the imagined utopia of the American dream requires a whole lot of work, so we think, *"When these kids get out of the house, when we move to warm weather and play golf all day, life will be wonderful!"* But then we reach the third

1

stage of life. Our homes are empty, and the aches and pains of age have set in. We're tired, we're lonely, and we think, *"I wish I could go back in time and life could be the way it was in my youth. I wouldn't be in such a hurry to get to where I am now."*

Or perhaps some of us are more aligned to the self-promotion life plan—those who imagine, *"If I get into the right school and have the right career, and make a lot of money, then I will be happy."* By God's grace, we get that dream job, and we realize we're spending more time trying to make a living than we are making a life. We get up, we work, we go to bed, and we start all over again. So we think, *"When I retire and have all this money set aside, then I can do whatever I want and I'll be happy."* But it could happen that one day we wake up in a small, sterile room, look back over our lives, and think, *"I wish I could go back to when there was more time. I would have those adventures I'd always wanted to go on but never got around to."*

I'm reminded of the last episode of NBC's hit sitcom, "The Office," a show about different people working in a mundane industry, experiencing the idiocycrisies of their diverse personalities and quirks. It's a situational comedy centered on something horribly bland—selling paper. In the final episode, a character named Andy Bernard delivers this terrific line: "I wish there was a way to know you're in the good old days before you've actually left them." [13] It's a telling statement that even when we feel we've advanced, a part of us longs to go back to an earlier time. The human heart is truly never satisfied on its own.

At some point, we must realize that maybe our hearts are made for something far deeper than a need for something or someone else to be added to our lives. We will continue to chase after what we hope will cure our emptiness until we receive the God who can satisfy us all in all.

LIFE WITHOUT GOD

The Hebrew word for vanity is *hăbêl*.[14] It's also a word that translates into "vapor, breath, or wind." Whatever its translation, it conveys a sense of fleetingness—of something being here one moment and gone the next.

What's the point, Solomon asks, of toiling tirelessly "under the sun" (Ecclesiastes 1:3) when life is nothing more than a vapor, a breath of air, or a wind? Those three description are key to understanding Solomon's perspective, because what he is saying is that he's looking at life horizontally, from a viewpoint that is purely humanistic. What is the value or purpose of life without God? The hard but simple answer is: not much.

When we examine the book of Ecclesiastes, we begin to understand Solomon is trying to lead us somewhere by living in our world, walking in our footsteps, and living the dreamlife. His experience shows us that maybe the people who have it all, and yet choose to end it all, are on to something—that you can get the whole world and still feel empty inside if you don't have God.

The point Solomon is trying to make is, without God, life and any of the joy it can bring is a vapor that's gone in an instant, leaving us empty once again.

Without God, Life Is Forgettable

A generation goes, and a generation comes, but the earth remains forever. The sun rises, and the sun goes down, and hastens to the place where it rises.
—ECCLESIASTES 1:4–5 (ESV)

Interestingly, Ernest Hemingway's breakthrough novel, *The Sun Also Rises*, was written as a somewhat autobiographical portrayal of his life in Paris, as an expatriate who rubbed shoulders with the likes of fellow author F. Scott Fitzgerald. The book conveys the sense of emptiness and disillusionment members of his generation felt on the heels of World War I. Ironically, Hemingway used the very words of Solomon from Ecclesiastes 1:5 for the title of his debut novel.

As biographer Mary Dearborn notes, Hemingway told the story in such a way that "the reader is not to take away from the book any real belief in the values—or, mostly, the lack of them— of his characters, or even of the narrator, Jake Barnes." [15] You could say, Hemingway helped to infuse modern Western culture with the very sense of emptiness Solomon had expressed almost three thousand years prior.

If we're honest, each of us can have moments where we wonder if our lives make all that much of a difference. This is a tragedy Solomon spells out in the first part of Ecclesiastes, with epic insight. A few verses later, he adds, "There is no remembrance of former things, nor will there be any remembrance of later things yet to be among those who come after" (Ecclesiastes 1:11).

Five years after I graduated from college, I went back to visit my college campus. The buildings were the same. The ambient sounds and activity around campus were familiar. But I was shocked and amazed by how quickly the school itself had moved on without me. As I walked through the campus, there was no one I recognized. And no one recognized me. I was a nobody.

Life is like that. You come in as a freshman. Nobody respects you, and everyone's beating you up and telling you what to do. Then you become a sophomore. You become a punk, people still beat you up, but you've begun carving out a place for yourself. Then you're a junior. You think you know everything and you own the place—until you become a senior and everyone around you is trying to move you out to pasture!

We all want to make a difference and leave a lasting impression in our world, but Solomon essentially said, "Without God, you're just waiting to be forgotten."

At the time I began working on this project, the president of the United States was Donald Trump, arguably one of the most polarizing figures in recent American history. Regardless of how you feel about the guy, it's easy to say he's a president who won't soon be forgotten. But go back two hundred years or so, to 1819. Can you remember the name of the then-president without looking him up? Who was he? What was he known for? Was he loved? Was he despised? What difference did he make in the continuing formation of this nation?

The answer is James Monroe. He was the fifth president of the United States, and though he was living in America at the time leading up to the Revolutionary War, he was not one of the signers of the Declaration of Independence.[16] (For the record, yes, I had to look him up too.)

The point I'm trying to make is, just a mere two hundred years later, the most important person in the country at that time has been largely forgotten by the country he once led. He's got a Wikipedia entry, but not much else. That's life without God in a nutshell—a four-year college (or presidential) term. It's over before you know it, and then you're forgotten.

Without God, Life Is Redundant

The sun rises, and the sun goes down, and hastens to the place where it rises. The wind blows to the south and goes around to the north; around and around goes the wind, and on its circuits the wind returns.
—ECCLESIASTES 1:5–7

Routine is a part of life. You get up in the morning, you tackle the day, you come home, and then you go to bed so you can begin again tomorrow—over and over again. Solomon felt this same monotony, as we see in Ecclesiastes 1.

For a more modern example, you need only look to the fall season. Every year, millions of people get excited about the arrival of pumpkin spice. We have pumpkin spice coffee. Pumpkin spice pancakes. Pumpkin spice candles. We even have pumpkin spice hand soap. And every year, we act like it's something exciting and new! Then, after a few weeks, the spices and syrups disappear from the shelves and coffee bars to make room for Santa and all things peppermint. Then it's on to hearts and chocolate. And every year, the same cycle repeats.

I'm not in any way suggesting these things are bad. I'm just saying that there comes a point when you start to realize history seems to be on repeat. That's life apart from God. It's not new; it's redundant. A spinning cycle. A series of events that come and go and come again. Is it any wonder that for some, that redundancy eventually becomes unbearably empty?

Without God, Life Is Unfulfilling

All things are full of weariness; a man cannot utter it; the eye is not satisfied with seeing, nor the ear with hearing. What has been is what will be, and what has been done is what will be done, and there is nothing new under the sun.
—ECCLESIASTES 1:8–9 (ESV)

Solomon knew something everyone eventually comes to understand: there is nothing "under the sun" that hasn't been done before. Interestingly, after Ernest Hemingway was severely wounded in World War I, he confessed a similar attitude: "I figured it out that nothing could happen to me that had not happened to all men before me. Whatever I had to do men had always done. If they had done it then I could do it too and the best thing was not to worry about it."[17]

This sort of fatalism, rooted in seeing the human experience through a wide lens, can lead us to a self-destructive search for pleasure. We may then spend much of our lives stuffing everything we can into the internal void that is the constant companion of so many of us, hoping to fill it yet never being able to do so. We can stuff and stuff and stuff everything possible into it—food, drugs, sex, social media likes, you name it—hoping to fill that emptiness inside, but all this ends up creating is more emptiness.

Solomon was all too familiar with that practice. He had all the riches, all the cool toys, all the food and drink, and all the women in the world, but the one thing he learned from his experiences was that life without God is unfulfilling. He writes, "I said in my heart, 'Come now, I will test you with pleasure; enjoy yourself'" (Ecclesiastes 2:1 ESV). And he did. He went after all the pleasure he could get.

Scripture tells us Solomon had a total of seven hundred wives and three hundred concubines during his lifetime (1 Kings 11:3). Imagine *The Bachelor*,[18] where every night is rose ceremony night, and every night only one rose is given—but instead of going home, the ladies stayed there for the rest of their lives hoping to be the girl he'd pick the next evening. I can imagine, in our sex-infused society, such a life would be a dream come true for many young men. But can you imagine the endless drama television producers would mine from that household? Solomon was the ultimate Bachelor of his day, living the supposed dream of young men; yet, in the end, he said, "It's *hăbêl*. It's vanity. It's chasing after the wind."

Some of us are spending our days chasing after pleasure. We live for the weekend. We look forward to each party. We can't wait for the next "buzz." But guess what? Eventually, Saturday night gets old. Being hung over all the way through Monday morning loses its appeal. That's what Solomon was saying to us almost three millennia ago.

So, what did Solomon do after he was done chasing pleasure? He hit the books: "I turned to consider wisdom…. And I said in my heart that this also is vanity" (Ecclesiastes 2:12, 2:15 ESV).

This is a season of life many people find themselves in as they approach their thirties. They realize the party can't last forever, and if they don't have a degree already, they realize they need an education and a marketable skill. Yet, we're living in a time when we're seeing this is also a vanity. From the day they start kindergarten, kids are told that if they study hard and get into the right college, they'll grow up to be someone. All they've ended up being is extremely in debt, wondering why no one wants to hire them.

So they decide to make their own way in the world and pursue their passion as a side hustle or as an entrepreneur, an influencer, or an activist. Guess what? Solomon did the same thing: "I made great works. I built houses and planted vineyards for myself… Then I considered all that my hands had done … and there was nothing to be gained under the sun" (Ecclesiastes 2:4, 2:11 ESV).

Solomon was a man who chased everything we chase. He tried to fill his life with everything we try to fill our lives with. And long before the days of Google searches and Yelp! reviews, Solomon left behind his own one-star rating about his time on earth. He said, "I hated life, because what is done under the sun was grievous to me, for all is vanity and a striving after wind" (Ecclesiastes 2:17 ESV).

Without God, Life Gets Old

Is there a thing of which it is said, "See, this is new"? It has been already in the ages before us. There is no remembrance of former things, nor will there be any remembrance of later things yet to be among those who come after.
—ECCLESIASTES 1:10–11 (ESV)

Smart technology is everywhere. It's in our hands, it's in our homes, and it's anywhere we shop, eat, and recreate. We have smartphones. We have smart watches. And in September 2019, Amazon announced the Echo Loop, a smart ring you could wear on your finger to have access to its Alexa virtual assistant anytime or anywhere, without having to pull out your phone.[19]

You know the first thing that went through my head as soon as this was announced? *I want one.* But I knew that as soon as I got it, it'd get old and dusty. It would just be another thing that I had to keep, maintain, and clean up. Well, fast forward a year to November 2020. Amazon announced they were discontinuing the Echo Loop smart ring, but not to worry! They would be updating their Echo glasses frames, which they'd also announced at the same time as the ring in 2019.[20]

This won't be the first time we've seen smart glasses (anyone remember the Google glasses?), and it likely won't be the last. What's been done will be done again. *There's nothing new under the sun.* But wait! you might say. That technology *was* new. It wasn't all that long ago we didn't have any form of smart technology.

That's true. The gadgets themselves are new, but these gadgets just offer new ways of doing old things. More convenient? Sure. More fun? Yeah. But we're still doing the same things we've always done, just in different ways. And after a while, that excitement begins to wear off. The technology becomes old and commonplace, and that old, familiar emptiness that accompanies the thought "*What comes next?*" inevitably returns.

At the time of this writing, Facebook has announced the Metaverse, the ultimate self-fulfillment platform where you get to create your life from the ground up.[21] It's your chance to have it all—even if only digitally—and become the fullness of who you envision. Sadly, I think many will find that this, too, is *hăbêl.* I mean, what's sadder—being addicted to real gambling or to virtual gambling that doesn't involve any actual money?

WHAT'S NEXT?

*The blessing of the L*ORD *makes rich, and he adds no sorrow with it.*
—PROVERBS 10:22 (ESV)

You're probably thinking this is where I tell you everything you enjoy doing is wrong, right? That you should focus on reading your Bible, praying, and going to church, because that's the only thing God really cares about. That you should have a family and focus on raising those kids right. That you should have a job so that you can (gladly) give your tithes and offerings. And that you should avoid anything and everything that remotely smells of pleasure, because it's all sin and it's all worthless.

But that's not what I want you to take away from this at all. Remember, there are no easy answers in Ecclesiastes, because there are no simple solutions in life. This is why some of what Solomon writes seems contradictory. After writing about the emptiness of his pursuits, Solomon writes, "There is nothing better for a person than that he should eat and drink and find enjoyment in his toil. This also, I saw, is from the hand of God, for apart from him who can eat or who can have enjoyment?" (Ecclesiastes 2:24–25 ESV).

Are you ready for the first huge point he's going to make? Here it is: love, knowledge, possessions, pleasure—these things aren't wrong, but you must look at them from the right perspective. You've got to put them in their proper place.

The problem Solomon encountered is the problem our culture experiences daily. We forget the God who made us and gave us all that we have. We take the blessings and forget the Blesser. We ignore the source of our truest satisfaction and elevate lesser things to the place of ultimate goal. Whether in education, occupation, or relationships, the human heart is "a perpetual factory of idols," [22] taking a secondary thing God gives us and making it the first thing we serve. Then, having sidelined the Author of Life from our existence, we grow up to find that something is still missing. We experience the emptiness of King Solomon.

When God is placed first in your life, secondary things (romance, work, family, success, hobbies, etc.) find their space around Him. If you take nothing else from this chapter, take away this: life with God is the *beginning* of wisdom, work, success, and (yes) even pleasure, not the end of them. When you put God first in your life, He can add to your blessings.

If you're struggling with emptiness—if you're wondering, *"What is the point of it all?"*—I would ask you to consider: where have you placed God in your life? Is He the first thought or the afterthought?

James wrote that if you lack wisdom, you should ask God (James 1:5). God is the source of wisdom; when we seek wisdom through Him, we will have success (see Joshua 1) and we will know pleasures that are *forevermore* (Psalm 16:11 ESV). Despite what the world would have you believe, life with God at its center isn't boring. He doesn't want you to be miserable. We know this because centuries later, Solomon's descendant Jesus came on to the scene and said pretty much the same thing, just with different words:

Don't worry about these things, saying, "What will we eat? What will we drink? What will we wear? These things dominate the thoughts of unbelievers, but your heavenly Father already knows all your needs. Seek the Kingdom of God above all else, and live righteously, and he will give you everything you need.
—MATTHEW 6:31–33 (NLT)

A life filled with worry and striving to find fulfillment and meaning is a life lived under the sun without God. What God is saying in this scripture is, *"Get to know who's over the sun, and everything under the sun will find its true light in your life."* Let Him be the anchor, the rock, the foundation that supports your life, and everything else will be held together in Him.

Do you know why so many people are empty? Because they're trying to fill their world with everything but the One who loves them unconditionally. It's like putting tires and a fresh coat of paint on a car with no engine. Sure, it looks shiny and new, but it doesn't get you anywhere further than a few likes on Instagram.

YOUR EMPTINESS CAN BE FILLED

This is the good news: there's a way to truly fill your emptiness. But the hard part is coming to realize you need it. Some of you are going to put this book down, go back to the "good life" pursuit, and sink yourself into romance, schoolwork, real work, or busywork, trying to fashion the perfect image of your life. But God offers you an alternative—to sink yourself *in Christ.*

Did you know that Scripture rarely refers to us as Christians? In fact, the word only shows up three times in all the Bible. The most common term for Christians in the Bible is "in Christ." Who are we? We are people *in Christ.* Do you know why that phrase is so important? It means that you come *into* the acceptance and approval and the pleasure of the Father. You are clothed in Christ, and what does God say to Christ as he comes out of the waters of baptism? "This is my beloved Son, with whom I am well pleased" (Matthew 3:17).

If you're in Christ, He says that to you: "*This is My child, with whom I am well pleased.*" And God said this before Jesus began His ministry. From this identity as God's Son, Christ worked for us so that we could enter into what He has in His Father.

The weekly rhythm testifies to the principle of which I speak. The spiritual day of rest changed when Christ came. Under the Old Covenant, the people of Israel worked six days to get to that final day of rest (day seven). But in Christ, we have entered the rest of Christ's work accomplished for us. Jesus declares on the cross, "It is finished" (John 19:30), or *tetelestai* in Greek, meaning "to bring to a close, to finish, to end."[23] Now, instead of working six days to get to rest, we rest on day one, Sunday, when most Christians gather to worship Him for His finished work. Then we work the rest of the week *from* that rest we have received in Him.

This is what separates the Christian gospel from every other religious or secular pursuit in life: we don't work to get there, and we don't define ourselves by arriving there. No, we rest in His work to bring us to Himself and then enter into the work He has for us, knowing the end result does not define us. Now you work as a beloved child of the Most High God, who promised Solomon through David, "I will not take my steadfast love from him [you]" (1 Chronicles 17:13 ESV).

I know of what I speak, because this true for me. And it can be true for you.

WORKBOOK

||||||||||||||||||||||||||||||||||||||

Chapter One Questions

Question: Describe a time in your life when you looked forward to something that eventually came about in your life (a school, a job, a relationship, etc.). What happened when you reached what you previously looked forward to? Is there any pattern you notice when it comes to your desires in life? Why do you think this is?

_____

_____

_____

_____

_____

_____

_____

_____

_____

_____

_____

_____

Question: What are your life pursuits? Are you chasing after a life that will leave a lasting impression? What do you think people will remember you for in five, ten, twenty, or fifty years? What do you want people to remember you for after you pass away? Do your current choices reflect that desire?

_____

_____

_____

_____

_____

_____

_____

_____

_____

_____

_____

_____

Journal: Get honest with yourself and with God. What do you think will fulfill you? What are you spending your time, energy, and resources on? When you honestly look at your life, what does it reveal about where your priorities lie?

_____

_____

_____

_____

_____

_____

_____

_____

_____

_____

Action: Have you ever considered yourself "in Christ"? Are you aware that God has saved you **only** by grace through faith in Christ's work, or are you still working to find an identity based in your own pursuits? Evaluate if God is in the right place in your life, and if not, ask Him to show you what changes you need to make in order to put Him first.

_____

_____

_____

_____

_____

_____

_____

_____

_____

_____

_____

_____

Chapter One Notes

CHAPTER TWO

|||||||||||||||||||||||||||||||||||||||||||||||||||

Living in the Space Between

For everything there is a season, and a time for
every matter under heaven...
—ECCLESIASTES 3:1 (ESV)

On December 6, 1965, the band known as the Byrds released their single, *"Turn! Turn! Turn!"* [24] It was an immediate hit and went on to top the charts, gaining the number one position on U. S. Billboard Hot 100. [25] Their hit song was a cover of American folk singer Pete Seeger. However, the song goes back even further than that—nearly three thousand years back, actually.

If you look up the lyrics and compare it to your Bible, you're going to find that it has been taken word for word from Ecclesiastes 3. [26] (Do we give God royalties?) Regardless of what version you listen to or which translation you read, it's a beautiful song because they're beautiful words. They resonate with us.

These words, as we discussed in the previous chapter, come from Solomon during his years. It was a time when he looked over the years of his life and asked himself, "What is the point?" If you're not there now, there's coming a day when you'll ask the same question of your life. And when you come to this juncture, you also come to the realization that you're not the center of the universe any more than the earth is the center of the solar system. (This was first proven by a smart guy by the name of Copernicus.) [27]

If you think about it, the very structure of the solar system we live in depicts how God designed us to live our lives. And when you come the revelation that you are not the end-all-be-all and that you were actually created to revolve around Jesus (the Son), it's a beautiful place to be. Because that, my friend, is when the emptiness of a life apart from Christ starts to dissipate and you begin to find your true meaning and purpose.

THE SOVEREIGNTY OF GOD

A lot of people believe in a Higher Power, but that doesn't mean they believe in the God of the Bible. What is amazing about the Bible is that it isn't a book; the Bible is a collection of books written by sages, wisemen, prophets, leaders, poets, kings, and paupers over 1,500 years of history. And they all point to one Being dwelling over all and above all, yet choosing to reveal Himself to us.

The Bible is about Jesus, the incarnation of God Himself coming down to earth to lead us back to Him. There's nothing vague or ethereal about the God it describes. It gives us example after example of *specifics*.

The book of Ecclesiastes shows us what life looks like apart from God (empty) and what life looks like with God (full). But what aspects of God make life *full*?

The sovereignty of God means that He is absolutely above all and in control—that nothing in your life happens without Him being in charge of it. Now understand, this doesn't mean that God necessarily makes everything happen in your life. In fact, He doesn't. What it means is that God is over everything that happens in your life. He sees *from* heaven everything that happens *under* heaven from beginning to end. And from His vantage point, He saw you before you were even conceived (Psalm 139:13–15).

Regardless of what you may have been told, there's no such thing as an illegitimate child. There are plenty of absent parents, but not a single person—including you—is an accident, a mistake, or a secondary thought. You are precious to God, and He makes your life full because He is sovereign over the events that you experience, both the pleasant and the unpleasant. When things happen in life that we don't understand or can't seem to make sense of, He can.

LIVING BETWEEN THE WOWS AND WHYS OF LIFE

For everything there is a season, and a time for every matter under heaven: a time to be born, and a time to die; a time to plant, and a time to pluck up what is planted; a time to kill, and a time to heal; a time to break down, and a time to build up; a time to weep, and a time to laugh; a time to mourn, and a time to dance.
—ECCLESIASTES 3:1–4 (ESV)

It took me a few rereads before I realized the list of events in Ecclesiastes 3 is a list of opposite extremes. He begins with birth and death; he ends with war and peace. In the middle, you find love and hate, as well as gathering and discarding, which in Hebrew is also a euphemism for friendship.[28] In other words, there is going to be a time to make new friends and a time when you'll have to say goodbye to old friends. The list goes on.

Look closely at verses 1 through 8 and you'll find a total of fourteen opposing pairs of extremes. This was done on purpose. Solomon doubled the number seven—which represents God's number of completion—and indicated there was something important to which he wanted us to pay attention.

In these verses, you see what all our lives look like no matter when or where we're born. On one side of the extreme are the things we love—I call them the "wows" of life. On the other side of the spectrum are the things we absolutely *don't* love. We hate these things. I call them the "whys" of life. What he points out is that life is going to fill you with a lot of things, from extreme to extreme, and these extremes simply bookend everything that happens in between. Ultimately, what Solomon says here is that there is a reason and a season for everything that happens in your life.

Sometimes you'll be on one end of the spectrum, where you're loving life and things are going well (wow!). Other times, you'll be on the end of the spectrum where you're hating life and nothing seems to be going well (why?). But the rest of the time, you'll be somewhere in the middle. We live between the wows and the whys of life.

I can still remember in vivid detail one of the great wow moments of my life. I'd just walked into our apartment after only being married for two months, and my darling wife Cheryl had left the positive pregnancy test on the coffee table. I remember sitting down, looking at it, and thinking, *"Wow. Life's going to be different now."*

And what a beautiful wow. My daughter is in college now, and I think *why* is college so expensive? I don't regret having her for an instant, because she is a delight in our lives. I thank God for the positive pregnancy test and for all the wows and whys that followed it.

What was your latest wow moment in life? Maybe it was an answered prayer, or an unexpected job offer, or seeing the one who would become your future spouse for the first time. When you feel it, you want to hold on to that moment forever. But life doesn't stay in the high, towering mountain of wow forever, does it? Sooner or later, it brings us down to the valley of whys.

"Why did the marriage end?"
"Why did that job not last?"
"Why am I not married?"
"Why can't I have a baby?"
"Why did that have to happen?"
"Why did they have to die?"

Life gives you wows, and life gives you whys. In this passage, Solomon shows us that it's unwise to focus too highly on either one, because you're going to live a lot of these moments and there's a time and a season for each. If we get too fixated on either extreme, it can heighten our sense of emptiness.

LIFE WITH GOD

If your focus is only on the events of your life, rather than looking to the One who is overseeing the events of your life, your perspective will eventually begin to warp. Instead of seeing all the wows, you'll begin to focus on all the whys. The more you focus on the whys, the more pointless and empty everything begins to feel. And before you know it, you've slipped into a depression.

In Ecclesiastes 3:16–17 (esv), Solomon writes:

> Moreover, I saw under the sun that in the place of justice, even there was wickedness, and in the place of righteousness, even there was wickedness. I said in my heart with regard to the children of man that God is testing them that they may see that they themselves are but beasts.

Understand what Solomon was saying. He was not saying we are beasts. He was saying that when left to our own devices, we act just like animals. It just takes a few minutes of scrolling on your phone reading the headlines to ask yourself, *"Why are people like this? Why are they so nasty to someone who looks, or thinks, or votes differently from them?"*

Things were no different back in the "good ol' days." When Solomon looked around him, he saw the vileness of humanity living apart from God.

> *Again I saw all the oppressions that are done under the sun. And behold, the tears of the oppressed, and they had no one to comfort them! And I thought the dead who are already dead more fortunate than the living who are still alive. But better than both is he who has not yet been and has not seen the evil deeds that are done under the sun.*
> **—ECCLESIASTES 4:1–3** (ESV)

It is estimated that approximately 6.3 million children under the age of fifteen die every five seconds in our world from preventable causes.[29] There is oppression, and the people in power don't hold the oppressors to account; instead, they exploit the very people they're meant to protect.

If you live long enough under the sun, you're going to find yourself gravitationally pulled into the whys, or maybe into the wows. They are momentary. Both the great and terrible times of your life are instants that slip through your fingers. You aren't made to live *for* them; you're made to expect them and to walk through them, with God as your constant companion. Living for the wows and whys can bring you, sooner or later, to the point where you don't want to live under the sun anymore.

Before he died by suicide, famed celebrity chef Anthony Bourdain would travel from exotic place to exotic place experiencing the food and culture, followed by a television crew to capture it all. He was adored by millions of fans for this work. In one particular episode in Vietnam, he was eating something and exclaimed, "Fellow travelers, this is what you want. This is what you need. This is the path to true happiness and wisdom." [30]

Yikes.

With no disrespect to his memory, those statements are just crazy talk. If you live for food, your life is a bittersweet series of momentary pleasures followed by long periods of waiting—not to mention the many meals you will *not* enjoy along the way. The "wows" are moments, but they can't provide meaning. Be careful, romance addicts, adrenaline junkies, Instagram influencers, and people who crave the applause of a crowd! These things only last for minutes or hours at the most, and they are few and far between; then real life comes roaring back. So many people take the place God should occupy in their lives and substitute something far more temporal and empty for His presence. Thankfully, there's an alternative approach to these extremes, which Solomon offers us to help reshape our perspective.

With God, There's a Season for It

For everything there is a season.
—ECCLESIASTES 3:1

When we live our lives focusing on everything *under* the sun, the question becomes, "What's the point of all this?" (see Ecclesiastes 3:9), so Solomon brings us back to the viewpoint of what's *over* the sun. He says, "Listen. This is how you've got to view whatever you're in right now. *For everything there is a season.*"

I am from New England. New Englanders understand seasons. In New England, there are at least twelve seasons. And what gets them through the many cold, bleak winters they experience in a single calendar year is the prospect of spring. They know the snowstorms and sleet and ice aren't going to last forever. But when March 20, the first day of spring, comes and there are still three feet of snow on the ground, they might think, *"Is it really going to happen?"*

Well, it does. Every year, spring shows up right on time—on July 1, followed by summer on July 3. (You have to be from New England to fully appreciate that statement.)

What we have to realize is that the seasons are speaking to our spirits. You might be in the season of asking "why?" right now, and God's word to you is this: "Don't freak out. This isn't permanent. It's a season."

I remember one of the worst seasons of my life. I was in a job where I was the only outsider; the rest of the employees were all relatives, and I was physically and emotionally bullied every single time I stepped through the door. I was shoved into closets and locked in storage containers for hours while I was supposed to be working, and I was mismanaged several times. I came home from work one day feeling depressed and defeated because I was tired of being treated as if I were a nothing.

My dad, who worked sixteen-hour days every day of his life, saw me sitting there at the kitchen table looking dejected and asked me what was wrong. So I told him. And I'll never forget his kind, compassionate words. He looked at me and said, "Tim, grow up."

He didn't coddle me. He didn't protect me. He didn't get on the phone and call the boss to try to fight my battles. Instead, he let the season serve me well. And I'll tell you one thing, I look back on my life now and I see that horrific job was one of the *best* worst seasons of my life. I would not trade it for anything in the world, because it taught me how to get tough when nobody liked me. I learned soon after, as a pastor, that some of God's sheep can bite, and if your skin is too thin, you'll never last. Thank God for skin-thickening seasons.

It's a very freeing season when you're hated, because when everybody hates you, you don't have to worry about what they think about you. Then you can finally become the person God really wants you to be, regardless of what people think of you.

I want you to highlight or underline this next statement: *embrace this moment as a season*. Write it on a sticky note and stick it on your bathroom mirror. Tell it to yourself when you feel like quitting. Seasons are designed by God to be periods of growth or rest as He *actively* prepares you for what comes next.

Thank God for these seasons. Because the "no's" and the "not yets" and the "whys" that you are experiencing right now are a gift from God. They are preparing you for the "yeses" and "nows" and "wows" that are coming for you!

With God, There's a Reason for It

I have seen the business that God has given to the children of man to be busy with. He has made everything beautiful in its time. Also, he has put eternity into man's heart, yet so that he cannot find out what God has done from the beginning to the end.
—ECCLESIASTES 3:10–11 (ESV)

More than a *season*, Solomon says that with God, there's a *reason* for everything you're going through. I want you to go back to Ecclesiastes 3:11 and underline the phrase *everything beautiful* in your Bible. If you need to, write the verse down on a 3 x 5 card and hang it somewhere you can see it the next time life is looking ugly.

This season you're in right now—whether it's a wow or a why season—is making you beautiful. Like a spiritual chemical peel, Jesus is using it to strip away the impurities and revitalize the soul, not to harm you but to make you beautiful.

Let me give you a scripture that we tend to brush right by, in Isaiah 55. The more you meditate on it, especially in light of the information we gain from science, the more it will blow your mind. The prophet says:

> For my thoughts are not your thoughts, neither are your ways my ways, declares the LORD. For as the heavens are higher than the earth, so are my ways higher than your ways and my thoughts than your thoughts.
> —ISAIAH 55:8–9 (ESV)

Look at the measurement God gives us to compare our thoughts to His thoughts: the distance from the earth to the heavens! Scientific studies have helped us understand just how immense that distance really is. The closest star to our planet, other than the sun, is Alpha Centauri, which is *4.75 light years* away. That means, traveling at the speed of light, it would still take you more than four years to reach it. The fastest thing mankind has created to travel space is Voyager I, which is headed toward Uranus traveling at 38,200 miles per hour.[31]

Now consider this: it would take Voyager I 77,000 years to reach Alpha Centauri from Earth! And God says that distance is about how distant your thoughts are from His. Life can seem confusing, even for Christians, when we are experiencing events we despise but God has a very different perspective. Yet, He knows far better than us what to do with our lives, because what we see is earthly, while what He sees is heavenly.

So please, stop telling yourself that you're all finished or ready to die. Stop telling yourself that you're not good enough. Stop telling yourself that you're a loser. Start telling yourself what Scripture says. You are being made more beautiful today, even if you don't like it right now.

Now go back to Ecclesiastes 3:11 and double underline this: *"He has put eternity into man's heart."*

God has placed something inside of us that resonates with eternity, which is why the temporary substance of this world never feels like enough. We long for more, for things eternal. We seek it. For many, we seek it in the wrong places—in jobs, in relationships, in status, and in all those other things we talked about in Chapter One. But the only thing that truly satisfies that longing in our hearts is Christ.

In 2019, one of the biggest headlines and topics discussed in churches across America was the conversion of Kanye West. He was flying all over the country, holding gospel concerts,[32] and the big question was, "Is this guy for real?"[33] In the October edition of *GQ* that year, there was an interview with Brad Pitt, who had attended one of Kanye's concerts. In that interview, Brad Pitt talked about his own spiritual journey, saying:[34]

I grew up with Christianity. Always questioned it, but it worked at times. And then when I got on my own, I completely left it and I called myself agnostic. Tried a few spiritual things but didn't feel right. Then I called myself an atheist for a while, just kind of being rebellious. I wasn't really. But I kinda labeled myself that for a while. It felt punk

*rock enough. And then I found myself coming back around to just
belief in—I hate to use the word spirituality, but just a belief in that
we're all connected.*

Brad called it *spirituality*, but I call it belief. He knows there's
something more. So do you. But it's not *something*; it's *Someone*.
Solomon writes that God has made all things beautiful in His time
and has put eternity in your heart. This is why you know there's
more, and long for more, to the point that it sometimes hurts in
the deepest parts of your being.

This is also why we need community (a.k.a., the church). We
need those outside reminders from our pastors and from our fellow
brothers and sisters that the things we're experiencing now aren't
going to last forever, and that God is still working in these experiences and through them. When we're drifting away in currents of
depression or despair, we need our community to come alongside
us and help pull us back to the shore of God's eternal promises.

Now comes the last and hardest part of verse 11: God has put
eternity into your heart, *but you can't picture eternity from beginning to end.*

Have you ever seen a real oriental rug? I'm talking the $10,000
dollar rugs. When you look at the front, you see a gorgeous picture that is fully complete, but if you flip it over, you see threads
going everywhere. It's chaos. It's a mess. It's a great example of
what life looks like for those of us living under the sun.

From our vantage point, all we can see are the threads running
here and there, without seeming to make much sense, but God,
who is above the sun, looks down and sees how all that chaos
on the backside produces beauty on the topside. He takes all the
messes and chaos of life and ties them all together, successfully
weaving every thread to make something beautiful at the end of

time. And when He comes back, all things will be made new; they'll be beautiful. Then we'll finally see what He's seen all along.

What Solomon is saying is that, yes, you know there is something more beyond this life, and you can know God has a plan and a purpose for your life, but you can't know it all from beginning to end. We get a glimpse of that beauty in life, yes. Just not the entire picture.

However, in the gospel, God offers us something even better than a glimpse. He offers us a Friend who walks through these seasons with us and gives us the faith to trust that these moments in time will ultimately be for our benefit rather than for our loss (Romans 8:28). Through Him, we have faith that one day, everything will be made clear (Romans 8:18–25)—and in Him, we'll finally see the beauty of it all.

WE FIND PEACE WHEN WE LEARN TO RECOGNIZE GOD'S SOVEREIGNTY

I perceived that there is nothing better for them than to be joyful and to do good as long as they live; also that everyone should eat and drink and take pleasure in all his toil—this is God's gift to man.
—ECCLESIASTES 3:12–13 (ESV)

Here Solomon returns from the why to the wow. He says that when you realize there is a God above it all, in charge of it all, bringing it all together, and beautifying it all, you don't have to worry about it all. You can get your joy back. He shows us that God's sovereignty over the seasons and reasons of life is our joy no matter the wow or the why.

Amy Carmichael was a missionary to India for fifty-five years.[35] As a little girl, she grew up in a neighborhood where almost all the other girls had blue, green, or hazel eyes. She remembered the Bible telling her that if she asked, she would receive, so she would pray every night before bed, asking God to give her blue eyes so that she would be pretty and more acceptable. When she woke up, she would go straight to the mirror to see if God had answered her prayer. Alas, no. Her eyes remained brown.

Her mother would talk about hearing Amy wail from her room every morning—for years—when she'd discover that once again, God had said no to her prayer for blue eyes.

In her twenties, Amy went overseas to reach India for Christ. When she got there, she found out that Indian women were selling their daughters to serve as temple prostitutes when they were as young as twelve years old. She knew someone had to go in and rescue them. Every morning, she got up and used coffee grinds on her face to darken her skin; then she dressed herself in the local garb, go into the temples, and rescue women and young girls who were being used as sex slaves. She rescued over one thousand women through her organization.

One day while applying the coffee grinds, she looked in the mirror and realized all the Indian girls had brown eyes. If God had ever answered her prayer to give her blue eyes, she never would have been able to blend in with the other people there, meaning she wouldn't have been able to rescue all those girls. Amy found joy in the sovereignty of God even when His sovereign answer was "no."

Moving into our own century, we see story after story of Black Americans dying because someone saw them and feared them. On September 6, 2018, a young man named Botham Jean was eating ice cream in his apartment when Amber Guyger, an off-duty police officer, walked through the wrong door and, thinking there was a burglar in her home, shot and killed him.[36]

It's natural for our hearts to cry out in anguish when we see injustice running rampant in our society. It's natural for us to demand answers when evil and senseless acts of violence steal our loved ones away. But Botham's younger brother, Brandt Jean, chose to look up rather than down in his grief, and his response showed us how quickly the whys in our lives can be come wows.

At Amber's sentencing hearing, a year after Botham's murder, Brandt Jean shocked the world when he spoke directly to his brother's killer and, instead of condemning her, forgave her.[37] Not only that, but he also pleaded with her to seek the love of Christ, who alone could heal her soul and bring her peace.

On that day, as Brandt stepped down from the stand and embraced Amber in a hug, he showed the world what Solomon was trying to teach us in Ecclesiastes 3: unless we who live under the sun reach out to the One living over the sun, we will never know contentment. And if you're watching the same world I am, you know we need peace now more than ever.

WORKBOOK

IIIIIIIIIIIIIIIIIIIIIIIIIIIIIIIIII

Chapter Two Questions

Question: What are some of the extremes you have experienced in your life (both that made you love and made you hate life)? How do you feel in the in-between moments? Why do you think that is?

_____

_____

_____

_____

_____

_____

_____

_____

_____

_____

Question: Have you ever felt like life wasn't worth living? What experiences led you to that point? What shift in your perspective can you make to approach life differently and overcome this kind of hopelessness? What attitude about life does God want to give you?

_____

_____

_____

_____

_____

_____

_____

_____

_____

_____

_____

Journal: Are you in a season of "why?" right now. Use God's word and spend some time in prayer listening for His voice. Journal a message of consolation, based on Scripture, from God to you. Whether you are in a season of "why?" right now or not, you can use the message from this exercise anytime you are in a season when you need encouragement from God.

_____

_____

_____

_____

_____

_____

_____

_____

_____

_____

Action: Use the phrases "Embrace this **moment** as a **season**" and "He has made **everything beautiful** in its time—Ecclesiastes 3:11" to create a tangible reminder for yourself. You can write them on 3 x 5 note cards and pin them on a bulletin board, set them on your desk, or stick them on your fridge with a magnet. Or you can get more creative with it: make these phrases your smartphone lock screen, create art with them, print them on paper and frame them, or use them any other way you are inspired to. The main point is to display these reminders where you will see them and be reminded of the hope God provides for you in every season.

_____

_____

_____

_____

_____

_____

_____

_____

_____

_____

_____

_____

Chapter Two Notes

|||||||||||||||||||||||||||||||||||||||||||||||||||||||||

_____

_____

_____

_____

_____

_____

_____

_____

_____

_____

_____

_____

_____

_____

_____

_____

_____

_____

_____

_____

_____

_____

_____

_____

_____

‖‖‖

God's Answer to Occupational Hazards

L ike most people born under the sun, your time on earth will be defined largely by the work you do during your lifetime. More than pleasure. More than love. More than family. You will spend far more of your time on this planet trying to make something of yourself through your career than anything else.

Back in 2015, MSN put together a prospectus about how much time we'll spend on average engaging in specific daily activities if we live seventy-five years.[38] Based on the collected research, they found that men will spend roughly 4 days of their life getting ready each morning; that number jumps up to 13 days for women. We will spend one year of our seventy-five years deciding what to wear (again, that number jumps up to two years for the ladies). We'll spend twenty-seven days waiting for mass transit, cabs, or Ubers. We spend three years of our lives washing clothes. (Thank goodness for the machines that do the heavy work for us!)

We will spend two years in meetings, but only four months will be spent laughing. If you think that's sad, you can bank time on the five months of your life you'll spend complaining about something. Of those seventy-five years, a whopping *twenty-seven days* will be spent on romance. So much for all the loves songs, romantic comedies, and fairy tales.

In the end, the article found that the top four time-takers in your life are shopping (eight years), watching television (ten years), sleeping (twenty-six years), and work (an estimated eleven years). If you're doing the math, that's roughly 96,360 hours punching a clock in your lifetime.

Considering this statistic, is it any wonder we largely define ourselves by our work? A 2014 Allstate-National Journal Heartland Monitor Poll said 71 percent of baby boomers insisted that achieving success in a career is necessary to living a good life, compared to 91 percent of millennials.[39] That's a 20 percent increase over the span of just a few generations. And when we meet someone new, the most commonly asked question we ask after learning someone's name is, "What do you do for a living?"

Work can consume us. It is where we often search for a sense of purpose and contentment.

Solomon understood work. He was known as Israel's premier construction project manager. He spent seven years building the temple of God. The workers for the temple alone comprised 80,000 stone cutters, 70,000 laborers, and 3,600 foremen. He spent thirteen years building his palace. He built a fleet of ships. He had stables of horses that he imported and exported. And he could sum up all of his labors in two verses:

I made great works. I built houses and planted vineyards for myself. I made myself gardens and parks, and planted in them all kinds of fruit trees. I made myself pools from which to water the forest of growing trees. I bought male and female slaves, and had slaves who were born in my house. I had also great possessions of herds and flocks, more than any who had been before me in Jerusalem.

—ECCLESIASTES 2:6–7 (ESV)

If we look only to our work to fill us, we are left wanting. Solomon spent three chapters talking about work in Ecclesiastes (chapter 4 to 6). His big take-away was that happiness, fulfillment, and contentment don't come *from* work alone, but *through* the work God gives you to accomplish.

WORK IS GOOD AND FROM GOD

The LORD God took the man and put him in the garden
of Eden to work it and keep it.
—GENESIS 2:15 (ESV)

I want to correct something that too many people mistakenly believe about work. They think of it as part of the curse. But as we see in Genesis 2, that is simply not the case. Work came into the garden of Eden before sin came into the world.

You were made to work. It doesn't matter if you're male or female; you were created to work in and among God's creation. When God created Adam, we read that it was to "work it and keep it." But He also knew that Adam needed a partner to work alongside him as he cared for the land and the animals, so He created Eve (Genesis 2:18, 2:21–22). When we go back to Genesis 1, which sums up all of creation, we see God surveying everything He'd made (and the purposes for each). He called it "very good" (verse 31).

Solomon backs this up in Ecclesiastes 2:24 (ESV) when he writes:

There is nothing better for a person than that he should eat and drink
and find enjoyment in his toil. This also, I saw, is from the hand of God.

Genesis 1 tells us that we are made in God's image and all of creation was an act of *work*. It was a good thing. We were intended to use the creation for our good and for the flourishing of all humans. We were also intended to work in partnership with God. Our work was designed to be fulfilling and beautiful, just like everything God had created prior to placing humanity in the garden. We were meant to create things with our hands, to look at what we've accomplished, and to say, "I made this. This is a good thing. A blessed thing."

But here's the problem. With one choice, sin entered the world; and like everything else sin touches, what was meant to be a blessing for us became a curse to us instead.

WORK IS CURSED BY SIN

Cursed is the ground because of you ... thorns and thistles it shall bring forth for you.... By the sweat of your face you shall eat bread...
—GENESIS 3:17–19

The curse comes in Genesis 3 after Adam and Eve have listened to the serpent instead of listening to God. When they followed the words of the serpent, they broke fellowship with God. They became *disconnected* from Him. Now, instead of work being something experienced in the form of a blessing from God, it has become something that is a frustration to us.

And because every human born since then has been born disconnected from God—and consequentially, disconnected from each other—instead of work side by side with others being the blessing God created it to be, it's become an irritation.

You read that right. The reason you are filled with a hopeless sense that you are toiling away for no reason in the workplace is because of sin.

Furthermore, because we are disconnected from God because of sin, we end up creating gods out of things that were never meant to have that status. When that happens, work become something it was never intended to be—the master of our lives, often at the exploitation or expense of those around us. This is where slavery comes from, where unfair employment practices come from, and where inequality and inequity come from. Instead of using creation to worship God and bless humans, we worship creation and use humans to serve us.

WORK HAZARDS

All of this theology bears witness in our lives through the types of frustration we experience in work. I call them occupational hazards—expressions of pain caused by the disharmony sin created in our relationship toward God, toward others, and toward work.

The Discontent Hazard

> Then I saw that all toil and all skill in work come from a man's envy of his neighbor. This also is vanity and a striving after wind.
> —ECCLESIASTES 4:4 (ESV)

I remember when I was in my senior year of high school. I had four friends who were all going to go into the pharmaceutical career path, which was a huge career in 1994. The promise was that after completing the college program, you'd make $60,000 a year.

Now, I had received a call in my heart to be a pastor at the age of thirteen. I'm an outlier; not everyone knows exactly what they're going to be when they grow up as a kid. That was God's grace to me. But if I hadn't known that being a pastor was what God wanted me to do, I know without a doubt I would have followed my friends into pharmaceuticals. I would have chased the $60,000 salary instead of going to Bible college and pursuing vocational ministry. I would have made a lot more money. But I would have been the world's most miserable pharmacist—or, perhaps, a pharmacy school drop-out.

Why? Because working in a pharmacy is not my calling. It's not what God created me for.

There are people who will choose a career path (a skill) based solely on what they see others doing and receiving in that field, and because they want that same blessing for themselves. Maybe someone becomes a lawyer not because they have a passion for pursuing justice, but because they want the lifestyle that they perceive comes with that profession—the cars, the clothes, the house, etc. Another person wants to be an actor, not because they have a passion for the craft, but because they want to be seen and recognized as being a *somebody*. That's not pursuing your calling; that's just plain old envy.

If you're in a place where you're trying to decide on a future career path, consider your motives for pursing it. If you're in a place where you've been working a certain job that you absolutely hate for years, consider your motives for staying there.

You must be careful that you don't chase after some "promised life" that's based on wanting what someone else has. If you do, you might give your life to a career or an occupation that you weren't made for. And you'll wake up every morning wondering why you aren't happy. You will become keenly aware of just how empty this life is.

Here's the short answer for that: it may be because you chased after the work God designed for someone else instead of looking for the work that God designed for you. And here's a secret I've learned in my years of ministry: when you're passionate about something, you find joy in the doing. The money, accolades, and every other shining bobble trail after. Don't chase the money. Chase what you know you're called to do, even if it doesn't pay! Why? Because God has a way of working through all your experiences and efforts to bring you to the ultimate place He created you for.

I think of Joseph, who worked for his father (for no pay) keeping watch over his brothers. After they betrayed him and sold him into slavery, he again worked (for little pay) in Potiphar's house. His faithfulness and skill were on display, but so were his looks, and Potiphar's wife attempted to seduce him. When he rebuffed her, she cried rape and Joseph was sent to jail as an innocent man. In prison, he worked for the warden faithfully and skillfully, once again for no pay. *Yet,* every step of the way, the "LORD was with Joseph" (Genesis 39:2, 39:21, 39:23). And in a matter of time—through the wows and whys of life—Joseph became prime minister of Egypt overnight (for great pay).

Joseph teaches us what Solomon reminds us: trusting God through it all by working hard at what He's given you—even if it means working two jobs, surrounded by people you wouldn't choose, and getting treatment you don't deserve—eventually finds you where He wants you.

We aren't living in the times of Joseph—no one can legally make us a slave—but life can have us wondering where it's leading. The one thing that keeps your feet grounded through the discontent is to know the Lord redeems the time and brings it all together.

The Dedication Hazard

Again, I saw vanity under the sun: one person who has no other, either son or brother, yet there is no end to all his toil, and his eyes are never satisfied with riches, so that he never asks, "For whom am I toiling and depriving myself of pleasure?" This also is vanity and an unhappy business.

—ECCLESIASTES 4:7–8 (ESV)

I don't know if you remember the movie *The Family Man*, starring Nicolas Cage.[40] Cage plays a New York playboy living the high life. But then things happen, and he gets a glimpse of what life would have looked like if he'd married his college sweetheart instead of breaking up with her. He spends the first half of the movie trying to figure out how to get back to his old life with the fast cars and the hot models, only to discover his true joy is being married to his sweetheart, changing all those messy diapers, and being surrounded by real friends. In the end, when he wakes back up in his old life, he leaves it behind to chase after the better thing.

This might sound counterintuitive, but it's true. You can get so dedicated to your career you never make time for relationships. You never build a home. You never create a life. And you find yourself empty and alone.

Solomon was saying here, "I've been there, and I've done that; learn from me." Work is good. It's designed by God to create good things. But don't abdicate the joys and the riches that God has for you in life for the sake of your career.

The "Difference Maker" Hazard

Better was a poor and wise youth than an old and foolish king who no longer knew how to take advice. For he went from prison to the throne, though in his own kingdom he had been born poor. I saw all the living who move about under the sun, along with that youth who was to stand in the king's place. There was no end of all the people, all of whom he led. Yet those who come later will not rejoice in him. Surely this also is vanity and a striving after wind.

—ECCLESIASTES 4:13–16 (ESV)

How many times have we heard someone say, "I just want to make a difference in the world"? Perhaps you've said it yourself. I'm not saying there's anything wrong with that, especially when you're pursuing a career that impacts the lives of others, such as vocations in ministry, teaching, health and human services, or even politics. But if you're entering into a field because you're hoping to do something that's remembered forever, you're striving for an empty thing.

In Chapter One, I asked if you could name the president of the United States in 1819 without looking him up. Unless you're someone who loves tucking away trivia and facts, you probably couldn't tell me. If you're like me, you might not remember the answer two weeks after looking that information up!

Fame and notoriety are a fleeting thing. Take William Hung for example. He auditioned for season 3 of *American Idol*.[41] His audition was so bad, Simon Cowell (who isn't known for his compassion) told the young man that he couldn't sing or dance, so there was no point in offering up any critique on his performance. Yet, despite Hung's inability to sing or dance, he actually got a record deal and went on to produce three records that sold over

100,000 copies. He appeared in three movies and went on sixteen talk shows. If you want to talk about getting everything you can out of fifteen minutes of fame, William Hung did it better than anybody else. And yet, he was a blip. Today, if you ask someone on the street who he was, you'll probably end up with a blank stare.

I only use him as an illustration to say, in the scope of eternity, no matter how high you climb the ladder of success, it always ends. Consider the last time you had this thought about a famous actor from a previous decade: "What ever happened to [fill in the blank]?" You know what happened? The world moved on. Their "difference" was temporary.

When you walk through life with the goal of making a difference, you have to watch out for the hazard of thinking that *you* are going to leave a lasting legacy in the world. If you fall into this trap, you risk sacrificing the things that matter—including your relationship with God—trying to change the world, only to discover that all your striving leaves you feeling empty and broken instead.

Am I saying not to try to do anything about the state of the world? No. Not at all. I am saying that the best difference you can make is the difference God is making—bringing people into the light of Jesus Christ so hearts can be changed by the gospel and neighbors can love each other as the Holy Spirit indwells them. That's the difference you want to make, and that's the difference God wants to make. My ultimate advice here is this: Do not ask God to get on board with your plans. Instead, get on board with His plan for the world and you'll succeed through whatever life hands you.

The Dissatisfied Hazard

He who loves money will not be satisfied with money, nor he who loves
wealth with his income; this also is vanity.
—ECCLESIASTES 5:10 (ESV)

A recent report came out that exposed our tendency to never be satisfied with where we are financially.[42] In May 2021, three generations were asked what they considered to be "wealthy". The millennials said you needed a net worth of $1.4 million. Gen X said, "$1.9 million." And the boomers said, "$2.5 million." Can you see a trend? The older you get, the more you think you need to be considered wealthy. What happens to the millennials when they reach boomer age and, perhaps, arrived at that $1.4 million figure? I'm thinking what you're thinking: they will still consider themselves *not* wealthy! Solomon was right—if we love money or wealth, we will never be satisfied.

Now let me define what it means to "love wealth." I believe we love wealth when the amount we have is the measurement of our lives. When money controls our decisions about everything. Ask yourself a simple question: would you do a job you hate for double your income now, or a job you love for half your income now? Hard question, to be sure. But which way you bend in those answers exposes how much influence money has over your life. There will always be some amount of pressure on your life because of money, but too much makes us empty no matter how full we seem.

When our annual wages become the focus of our work, we fall into the trap of being dissatisfied no matter what we make. We're always wanting something more because we're never satisfied with what we have. We become bitter. We moan. We complain. And we're always looking for that next job that's finally going to pay us "what we're worth."

Solomon warns us of this in Ecclesiastes 6 (ESV) when he writes, "All the toil of man is for his mouth, yet his appetite is not satisfied" (verse 7). When our focus is on the *compensation* and *provision* resulting from our labor, we lose sight of the One who *compensates* and *provides* for our needs. Jesus says the same thing in Matthew 6:24 (ESV): "No one can serve two masters, for either he will hate the one and love the other, or he will be devoted to the one and despise the other. You cannot serve God and money."

One Master leaves you feeling satisfied and full no matter what your circumstances. Paul knew this more than most. Remember the dramatic prison break in Philippi in Acts 16, when he and Silas sang worship songs in the belly of that prison? He must have loved that moment. Not only was he vindicated as innocent, but the jailer was also reached with the gospel. But years later, Paul was in prison again, writing to the church in Philippi that formed as a result of that prison break in Acts 16. This time there was still joy and singing in Paul's life, but no dramatic supernatural prison break. What did Paul say? Perhaps some of the most famous and beloved words of Scripture: "I know how to be brought low, and I know how to abound. In any and every circumstance, I have learned the secret of facing plenty and hunger, abundance and need. I can do all things through him who strengthens me" (Philippians 4:12–13 ESV).

If Paul chased miracles and supernatural vindication, his life could have been considered a failure, because Nero eventually beheaded him. But Paul chased the Master of his destiny—the Lord Jesus Christ. Therefore, the ups and downs never held his heartstrings. He was *content* to be in the hands of the One who made him. And today, countless people quote his words, "I can do all things through Christ," when less-than-desirable events arise. Contentment in God is a powerful testimony.

The Disaster Hazard

> *There is a grievous evil that I have seen under the sun: riches were kept by their owner to his hurt, and those riches were lost in a bad venture. And he is father of a son, but he has nothing in his hand.*
> **—ECCLESIASTES 5:13–14** (ESV)

Be careful of defining your existence based on what you do. Economies rise and fall. Companies that are too big to fail become heaps of rubble. Housing bubbles burst. Pandemics sweep across the globe and shut entire countries down. Bad days can turn into bad weeks, and you might not hit those goals being expected of you. Given enough time, you might begin to think that because you're not living up to your job description, you're not any good at all.

> *...a man to whom God gives wealth, possessions, and honor, so that he lacks nothing of all that he desires, yet God does not give him power to enjoy them, but a stranger enjoys them. This is vanity; it is a grievous evil.*
> **—ECCLESIASTES 6:2** (ESV)

We live in a culture that often defines us by what we do. So we chase after careers that we think will give us value and purpose, and we pour everything we have into reaching the top of that career. But when a career and work is the god of your life, it has the capacity to destroy you.

Scripture tells the story of one such example in Herod Agrippa, in Acts 12. The chapter begins with Herod on the top of his game, having beheaded James, Jesus' disciple, and imprisoning Peter shortly thereafter. Then God went to work, sending an angel to deliver Peter from jail, to Herod's confusion. Herod responded by executing the guards who were responsible for Peter's imprisonment. He then decided to take his anger out on neighboring regions of Tyre and Sidon.

Herod took the stage and spoke, to great acclaim. The people under his rule celebrated and worshiped his words as "the voice of a god, and not of a man" (Acts 12:22 ESV). At that moment, Scripture and history confirm that Herod collapsed before them all and died.

Here was a man who had authority, success, and fame, not to mention the adoration of the people. But very quickly and without much fanfare, his life slipped into history, with no one really missing him. He had locked up the truth and puffed up his own ego, until one particular day under the sun when everything popped and deflated completely. Today we name our sons Peter and Paul, but I've only found one hotel in Tel Aviv named for this once-mighty politician.

When your life is defined by importance in the eyes of the world instead of investment in the purposes of God, history will not be kind to you. Consider, after all, that we call our salads Caesar but name our children Peter.

THE ANSWER TO THE HAZARDS OF WORK

Better is a handful of quietness than two hands full of toil and a striving after wind.
—ECCLESIASTES 4:6 (ESV)

Solomon gives us two suggestions about how to avoid the hazards of work. Solomon's first suggested defense against falling prey to the hazards of work is *contentment*. He says it's better to have peace about what cannot be stolen from us (a right relationship with God) than two handfuls of anxiousness trying to hold on to what we cannot keep (everything else).

For some of us, this is where we are. We've trying to get hold of everything we possibly can in life, squeezing every nickel out of every business deal and looking for the next best thing. But our heart isn't healthy. Our stress levels are through the roof. When we should be resting and sleeping, we're working overtime, trying to get ahead of our neighbor—or trying to prove to somebody that we're worth something because we've accomplished so much.

I think of all the children who are trying to out-shout the disapproval of their parents by making a name for themselves through their work and their toil. Their heart (physical and spiritual) is suffering as a result. I once heard Rick Warren say, "We spend the first fifty years of our lives sacrificing our health to get wealth, and then we spend the rest of our lives sacrificing our wealth to hold on to our health."

Paul wrote to Timothy that "godliness with *contentment* is great gain" (1 Timothy 6:6). Contentment is when you stop, turn around, and look at all the things God has given you, and you start to say, "Thank you." This is what the Bible calls praise and worship. Praising and worshiping the Giver of all good things will turn your spirit around in a moment, because it reminds you that you aren't facing the toil of your days alone.

Solomon's second suggested defense against falling prey to the hazards of work is *companionship*.

Two are better than one, because they have a good reward for their
toil. For if they fall, one will lift up his fellow. But woe to him who is
alone when he falls and has not another to lift him up! Again, if two
lie together, they keep warm, but how can one keep warm alone?
And though a man might prevail against one who is alone, two will
withstand him—a threefold cord is not quickly broken.
—ECCLESIASTES 4:9–12 (ESV)

When we look at Christ, we see that He had numerous friends and followers, but He had three *close* companions—Peter, James, and John. And out of those three, John was most likely His closest friend, leaning on His chest at the Last Supper and being given caretaker responsibilities over Mary at the foot of the cross. Jesus loved all people, but even He had close-knit friends.

If you look throughout the Bible, there's several places where this happens. David had his three mightiest men who were over his thirty mighty men. Earlier in David's life, Jonathan was his closest friend and confidant. Moses had Aaron, Abraham had Eliezer of Damascus, and Paul had a few men he considered sons and worthy partners in life—Timothy and Epaphroditus among them.

You've got to have people in your life. Don't chase career at the cost of friends, and choose which friendships you invest in wisely. I thought about Solomon's illustration of a threefold chord in terms of friendships, and this is what I walked away with: During the course of your life, you will have seasonal friendships and acquaintances. There will be good people who are a part of your life for a time, but eventually, you will part ways. There is great value, however, in having lifelong companions who walk through life's wows and whys with you. In the end, investing in those key relationships will yield greater dividends than any other option. You've got to have people in your life.

Solomon's two suggestions for us for avoiding the hazards of work are contentment and companionship, and God's ultimate answer is this: come to Me.

> *Guard your steps when you go to the house of God. To draw near to listen is better than to offer the sacrifice of fools, for they do not know that they are doing evil. Be not rash with your mouth, nor let your heart be hasty to utter a word before God, for God is in heaven and you are on earth. Therefore let your words be few.*
> **—ECCLESIASTES 5:1–2** (ESV)

God's not telling us to "go to church," but to consider how we go to church. Don't just walk into church carrying all the things you want God to do in your life and career. This is how we taint our experience with God. We come to Him and say, "I need this and that! I want You to help me with this problem or that challenge. Please give me what I need." Such anxiety-driven approaches will rob us of the opportunity to hear His voice.

We guard the way we enter God's house by learning to *listen first and speak second.* This is vital, because we must *come* to God before we can *hear* from God. And God has something to say that is better than anything you could come up with.

In the 1950s, there was a pastor of a very successful rural church in Pennsylvania. Every night, he would watch the *Tonight Show with Johnny Carson.*[43]

One day he had a thought: *"What if I sold the TV and spent that time just talking to God?"* He did it. And one day shortly after that, he saw *a Life* magazine cover of gang members in New York City. He felt God say to him: "Move to New York and help those boys." He did. He went to the first court case he could find and said he wanted to speak up for them. They kicked him out of the court. But he kept working the streets and preaching the gospel in the city. Eventually, he founded a ministry for drug-addicted persons and named it "Teen Challenge."[44] His name was David Wilkerson.

Today Teen Challenge is in 110 countries, with 1,100 centers to help millions of people escape the power of drugs and alcohol through Jesus Christ.[45] Countless lives have been saved by this ministry, and it all began because someone turned off the TV and listened to what God had to say.

I'm not saying you need to go out and start some huge movement, but imagine what God could do through you if you take the time to listen to what He has to say about your job and your career.

Secondly, we need to receive first and give second. Too many of us think that God just wants to take everything from us. My question is, why would the God who already owns everything need to take anything from you? In Ecclesiastes 5:4–5 (ESV), Solomon said:

> When you vow a vow to God, do not delay paying it, for he has no pleasure in fools. Pay what you vow. It is better that you should not vow than that you should vow and not pay.

God doesn't want us to bargain with Him, yet so often we come to Him with an attitude of, "God, if You do this thing for me, then I'll do that thing for You." We do this both consciously and unconsciously, and we develop the mentality that thinks God owes us something. God doesn't owe us a thing, but He wants to give us something that's precious to Him. Understand this: God is good. He's a giver. James tells us, "Every good and perfect gift is from above, coming down from the Father" (James 1:17 ESV). Yet, later in his book, he warns us clearly:

*What causes quarrels and what causes fights among you? Is it not this,
that your passions are at war within you? You desire and do not have,
so you murder. You covet and cannot obtain, so you fight and quarrel.
You do not have, because you do not ask. You ask and do not receive,
because you ask wrongly, to spend it on your passions.*

—JAMES 4:1–3 (ESV)

The lesson James and Solomon offer us is this: God gives, but
we must receive and share. There's a purpose to prosperity that's
greater than the temporary pleasure it brings.

JESUS FIRST, REST AT LAST

*Come to me, all who labor and are heavy laden, and I will give you rest.
Take my yoke upon you, and learn from me, for I am gentle and lowly in
heart, and you will find rest for your souls.*

—MATTHEW 11:28–29 (ESV)

In Matthew 11, Jesus speaks to all the busy bees and says,
"Come to Me and I will give you rest for your souls." I started
this chapter talking about how work has been cursed. And what is
that curse? Thorns, thistles, and the sweat of our brows. But two
thousand years ago, the Son of God became flesh, and He went to
the cross. Before He went to the cross, they put a crown of thorns
on His sweaty brow.

What man meant to use to mock Christ, God used to say,
"What Adam and Eve put you through, I'm bringing you out of.
What Adam and Eve subjected you to, I'm saving you from.

"And if you'll put your hope in Me, and you'll put your life in
My hands, I'll empower you to succeed. I'll empower you to rest.
I'll empower you to do what I want you to do. And your work will

not have to be the final definition of your life. You'll cross from this life into the next life hearing My voice say, 'Well done, good and faithful servant. Enter into the joy of heaven.'"

That's why Jesus went to the cross, and that's why He wore that crown of thorns: *so that you don't have to.* When we rest in the finished work of Jesus, our work no longer defines us and we are free to accomplish what God assigns us. And when you're in that space of doing what God has created you to do, emptiness doesn't stand a chance!

WORKBOOK

IIIIIIIIIIIIIIIIIIIIIIIIIIIIIIIIIIII

Chapter Three Questions

Question: How do you view work? Does it occupy an unhealthy place of focus in your life? What is God's view of work? How can you honor God with your work?

_____

_____

_____

_____

_____

_____

_____

_____

_____

_____

_____

Question: To which of the common work hazards do you find yourself most susceptible? Are any of these hazards currently affecting your relationship with work and God? What shifts do you need to make in order to make work fulfilling again?

_____

_____

_____

_____

_____

_____

_____

_____

_____

_____

_____

Journal: Write an explanation of how you believe contentment and companionship can help you avoid and overcome the common hazards of work. What specific, intentional choices do you need to make to begin pursuing contentment and companionship in that way?

_____

_____

_____

_____

_____

_____

_____

_____

_____

_____

_____

Action: Set aside some time to intentionally **rest** in the finished work of Jesus Christ. How long you do this is up to you, but devote this time to being free from work or distraction. Focus on God and His presence, and allow Him to bring the rest and contentment your soul craves.

_____

_____

_____

_____

_____

_____

_____

_____

_____

_____

_____

_____

Chapter Three Notes

llllllllllllllllllllllllllllllllllllllllllllllllllllllllllll

CHAPTER FOUR

IIIIIIIIIIIIIIIIIIIIIIIIIIIIIIIIIIIIIIIIIIIIIIIIIII

Long-Term Living in a Short-Term World

Wisdom is good with an inheritance,
an advantage to those who see the sun.
—ECCLESIASTES 7:11 (ESV)

I f you go to Google.com and type in "knowledge is," the first autofill that comes up is "knowledge is power," and the quote is typically attributed to Sir Francis Bacon.[46] But here's the most important thought concerning knowledge: will we use what we know for good or for evil? We live in an incredibly knowledgeable age. We know more about the universe and everything in it than ever before. With knowledge, we can learn about nuclear power and how to utilize it to power a city—which is good. And yet, with that same knowledge, we can (and have) used nuclear power to destroy a city—definitely not good.

The truth is, knowledge is amoral. You can learn everything there is to know about a subject without learning how to put that information to proper use. The old saying goes, "Knowledge is understanding a tomato is a fruit. Wisdom is not putting it in a fruit salad." I don't know where that saying comes from, but it's both funny and true. The difference between knowledge being used for good and for evil is wisdom. In Proverbs 2:6–8, Solomon explains that all wisdom comes from God. And in Paul's letter to the Colossians, the apostle writes that "all the treasures of wisdom and knowledge" are hidden in Christ (Colossians 2:2–3 NLT). Knowledge is fine. But knowledge without wisdom can be disastrous or disgusting—just ask someone who has ever tried tomato in a fruit salad!

This is the lesson Solomon is trying to teach us in the book of Ecclesiastes.

WISDOM SEPARATES GOD'S BEST FROM WHAT SEEMS GOOD

> *A good name is better than precious ointment, and the day of death than the day of birth. It is better to go to the house of mourning than to go to the house of feasting, for this is the end of all mankind, and the living will lay it to heart.*
> **—ECCLESIASTES 7:1–2** (ESV)

If you've ever tried to read through Ecclesiastes, you may have noticed that Ecclesiastes 7 marks the turning point of Solomon's memoir. Where the first half of the book describes what I like the call the "been there, done that" portion of Solomon's experience, the second half outlines the "now what?" portion of his life experience. Having described his eventual emptiness from chasing life, he then seeks to help the reader understand the way forward.

The first thing he's going to teach us is that life with God brings us the wisdom of God. Wisdom is what you need to live a meaningful, satisfying life—a life you will look back on at the end and say, "Good, I did meaningful things with the time and resources I was given by God."

I encourage you to take a moment to read through Ecclesiastes 7:1–14 in your Bible. As you read through it, underline or highlight every instance of the word *better* you come across.

As you look over your life, think about all the good things you've wanted at one point in time or another. How many times did you get that good thing and think it wasn't that great? Now think about a time you didn't get that good thing but eventually ended up with something *better* down the road. Something that you would have missed out on all together had you gotten that *good thing* right when you wanted it.

Wisdom helps us discern God's best from what seems good to us in the moment. Wisdom says, "Lord, I think this way, but what do You say?" We may think that if we get all the good things right when we want them, we'll feel happy and satisfied. But God's plan for us is so much better, even if it feels difficult in the moment.

The point Solomon makes in this chapter is that physical wealth and worldly knowledge means nothing apart from God's wisdom. But if you have wisdom, you can do much, whether you are physically rich or physically poor, whether you have that fancy degree from a fancy school or a certificate from a trade school. Because life is not about getting the most toys or accumulating the most wealth; it's about doing what is best with what God gives you.

It's not about what you know, but about what you do with what you know. It's not about where you're from, but what you do from here forward. Wisdom helps you discern when something that seems good is a lie. It also helps you to recognize what God's best is for your life.

Wisdom Prepares Us to Take the Hard Road

There is a way that seems right to a man, but its end is the way to death.
—PROVERBS 14:12; 16:25 (ESV)

There are moments in everyone's life when we're presented with something that seems good or feels good or looks good, but it turns out to be a disastrous thing. One of the biggest disasters that come to mind was the time a talking snake said that a certain superfruit would open the doors to humanity's full potential (Genesis 3). We all know how that turned out. Eve saw the fruit, and it *looked good,* so she ate it and gave it to Adam; but in the end, it brought only misery, destruction, and death.

Modern society is living in an escapist generation, where we rush to grab anything that looks good and turn away or reject anything that makes us unhappy or uncomfortable. We work for the weekend. We binge-watch an entire TV season or series in the space of a few days. We fill up digital shopping carts with the latest "must haves."

The world has programed us to choose the *easy* now without thinking of the *hard* later. Even our diets teach us to do this. We choose the easy, fast, prepared, processed foods now and destroy our bodies and metabolisms, then wonder why we can't lose the extra pounds we're carrying around or why our doctor is having to prescribe yet another medication for us to take to keep our bodies in some form of working order. This mentality is one that often leads to addiction or bondage in some form, because what you think is an escape is actually becoming a trap in your life.

Be careful about what you turn to when things are turned against you. Be careful of where you're looking to bring your heart reprieve when you feel restless. Rest is important. But when you are in the midst of difficulties, you need to turn your eyes to Christ and learn how to stand firm, rather than turning to the outlets that the devil will offer you quickly in an attempt to distract you from the *better* thing that God has for you in this season.

One of the best pieces of wisdom I received for sustained progress in my career was to intentionally create a space of recreation. So I picked up several different hobbies over the years that have nothing to do with my occupation. I rollerblade, play tennis, and 3D print on a regular basis. I also spend time making music that I never release for public listening. Why? Because that is my private space of "play"—recreation. I was told the reason to create a space of recreation is because if we do not create this space, the devil will create one for us, and his spaces come loaded with addiction and tragic loss.

Wisdom gives you the strength to choose the *hard* now so that you can enjoy the *easy* later and in the *best* form possible.

Wisdom Grounds Us in Reality

See to it that no one takes you captive by philosophy and empty deceit, according to human tradition, according to the elemental spirits of the world, and not according to Christ.
—COLOSSIANS 2:8 (ESV)

Have you ever met a Christian who is so "spiritually minded they're of no earthly good"?[47] These are people who live in the clouds, always jumping from one emotional experience to the next. Christians can be famous for this. Always talking about how they can't wait to get out of here and get to heaven, without having any care about what happens here on earth. These people offer no benefit to the people they are living around. I call them "Detached from Reality" Christians.

The real world we live in is hard. The real world we live in is challenging. We must have real eyes for a real world and face life's hard issues with God's wisdom.

This is why I love the path Solomon is about to take us down as we work our way through the next several chapters. He walks us through the hard realities of the world, such as injustice, and if I could say thank you to Solomon for just one thing about the book of Ecclesiastes, I would say thank you for not giving us pie-in-the-sky theology. In other words, he doesn't sugarcoat the lesson—which is why many might be confused about the rest of Ecclesiastes. There are no "do this to get that" promises. There are no simple solutions. You're going to have to deal with less-than-desirable events and work or live in situations that offer no quick escape or simple solution. You're going to have to navigate life's mess without losing your mind. Herein lies the greatest gift the book offers.

ESTABLISHING OUR IDENTITY IN THE WISDOM OF GOD OVER THE LONG TERM

A good name is better than precious ointment,
and the day of death than the day of birth.
—ECCLESIASTES 7:1 (ESV)

When the Bible talks about names, it's talking about character—who you really are when everything else is stripped away. When you look at the names given to the men and the women in the Bible, most often you'll discover that their name matches a key element of their identity. *Elijah,* the name of the prophet who stood up against the evilest king in Israel's history, means "My God is Yahweh."[48] He didn't just reject the false gods being worshiped by his people; he went to war against them. *Solomon* means "Peaceable,"[49] and his reign was the only time in Israel's history when the kingdom grew through peaceful pursuits rather than through conflict.

In today's society, we typically pick names that we like the sound of, or that remind us of someone who was important to us. If you grew up with a kid named Peter who was a bully and a jerk, and your spouse said, "I like the name Peter" when discussing possible names for your son, your response wouldn't be, "That's a good name!"

No. You'd say, "I knew a Peter growing up, and he was a jerk. I'm not naming my son that."

Names matter. And the character associated with a name resonates with you for a long time, for good or for ill. This is why you've got to think about your character—who you're becoming—over the long term. However, you're living in an age that increasingly demands you make a name for yourself in the immediate and in the short term. And this is poison to your soul. The following is just one example of this:[50 51 52]

In 1997, at age nine, he sold a million records.

In 2000, at the age of twelve, he sold another three million records.

In 2003, at the age of fifteen, he filed for legal emancipation from his mother.

In 2006, at the age of eighteen, he was engaged to a Playboy model for a week.

In 2008, at the age of twenty, he was arrested for marijuana possession.

In 2013, at the age of twenty-five, he filed bankruptcy to shed $3.5 million in debt.

In 2017, at the age of twenty-nine, he was arrested for DUI and was shrunk to a malnourished weight of 115 pounds after being on a dangerous combination of prescription medications.

And while writing this book in 2022, I turned on the news and saw: he died. After battling what one news outlet called "multiple mental health issues, including multiple personality disorder, schizophrenia, acute anxiety and manic depression," he was found dead in his bathtub.[53] How utterly sad.

His name was once in lights: Aaron Carter. He rose to fame in an instant, and the world chewed him up and spit him out before he was thirty.

Aaron's name in the year 2000 was admired and usually appeared somewhere in lights. But today his name is in an entirely different category. Why? Because sometimes quick-hit living leads to long-term disaster.

Now, let me promise you: God does *not* want that for His children. He's taking us down the long road, empowering us to choose the *best* options and handle the *hard reality* of life. The question is: how can we aim for the long term when everyone around us seems so enamored with the short-term, fast-rise, accomplishment-driven mindset? A few wise lessons from Solomon follow.

Long-Term Living Seeks to Make Investments

It is better to go to the house of mourning than to go to the house of feasting, for this is the end of all mankind, and the living will lay it to heart.
—ECCLESIASTES 7:2 (ESV)

Social media dominates our world. Sadly, it's dominating our minds in unhealthy ways. The research is proving again and again, we cannot continue to live healthy lives without understanding the dangers of this present obsession with likes, followers, and retweets/reposts.

Back in 2017, the Royal Society for Public Health published a study examining the effects social media is having on our young people.[54] In the study, they found that of the most popular social media platforms at the time, Instagram and Snapchat had the most negative effect on teens and young adults' mental and emotional well-being, while YouTube was the most positive of the platforms. More recently, a whistleblower accused Facebook and Instagram of engaging in practices that knowingly put young girls' mental and physical well-being at risk.[55]

The social media-oriented, impression-obsessed generation tends to post constantly about where they are and what they're doing in an effort to appear as if they're living their #bestlife 24/7. Many live their lives looking for affirmation in the number of likes, shares, and followers they collect. As a result, their entire identities are tied up in a momentary impression that offers no real or lasting payout in the end. And for far too many young people, the toll this impression-based lifestyle takes is their very lives.

Maybe this describes a struggle you're facing in your own life. If it is, Solomon is inviting you to look at the investments you are you making in your life.

It's easy to pose for a camera and add in special features that make you look great for the "right now" moment, but there's something more important—and that's your character. When Solomon says, "The day of death is better than the day of birth," he is not saying that death is better than life. He is saying the aim of your life is what is most important. This is why Solomon says to get yourself to a good funeral once in a while: because funerals give you a wake-up call that few other events in life will. Never once have I seen someone's possessions or social media results talked about at a funeral. No, there's conversation around the person's character and their positive influence on the lives of those around them! A funeral reminds us of the reality that someday we're going to be the one lying at the front of the chapel with people sitting around talking about the way they remember us. Make investments that matter for *that* moment.

What are you living for, and how are you living for it?

One of the most popular ways of describing ourselves today is, "I was born this way."[56] It's a concept that consciously or unconsciously claims that we are forever locked into whatever identity we were born with. Forever. That's not empowering or freeing. That's imprisonment and slavery. It's also short-sighted and closed-minded. You were born to learn, to grow, and to develop—to become something more than a simple product of biology and environment.

Let me tell you something. I was born a mess. You were born a mess, too. You were born with issues, selfishness, greed, envy—all of it. Sin nature has been a part of your DNA since the day you first drew breath. Your mom never needed to teach you how to steal a toy from someone else. No one had to show you how to say, "Mine!" But you did need someone to teach you how to share and how to get along with others. How you began life doesn't matter much in the scope of eternity. But how you end life does.

This is good news for anyone who is not proud of where they came from. It's good news for anyone who was raised outside of faith and who thinks that the sum of their life thus far excludes them from ever being used by God. Nonsense! With God, it's never about what you started out as; it's all about what you finish as. God can take the worst of sinners and turn them into a mighty man or woman to be used for His glorious purpose. This is the beauty of our faith—it's the resurrection faith, which takes what is dead and makes it alive!

John Newton lived a wretched life for most of his early years. His mother died when he was seven, and he followed his father's career path in merchant shipping. He was known for his "unsettled behavior and impatience of restraint," which cost him his first job. He sinned without abandon and sought to lead others to do the same. But one night, having experienced a storm at sea and while reading Thomas a Kempis' *An Imitation of Christ,* [57] he realized he was no true believer.

From that moment, he considered how to use his life to influence the world for good. He maintained a questionable position in the slave trade but grew more and more disgusted with the practice and finally quit. Eventually, he pastored a church in Olney, England, and with the poet William Cowper's help, put together some of the world's best-loved worship songs—among them, "Amazing Grace." He worked tirelessly for the rest of his life with William Wilberforce to *end* the slave trade once and for all. His life began enslaved to sin, but his later investments changed the world for good.[58] Had he never been converted by Christ, no one would know who he is. But today, he's remembered as a force for good, whose impact is still felt around the world.

When you live with a long-term perspective, you don't worry so much about temporary *impressions* you leave with strangers in your follower or friends lists, but you make *investments* in real people, with real help and real effort. In an age obsessed with impressing, wisdom calls us toward investing. I've got four investment tips that I recommend to net you the greatest eternal gains:

1. Absorb God's word. This is probably the most important investment you can make in your life. I'm not talking about listening to podcasts or reading study books (which do have a time and a place). I'm talking about taking time to sit down and immerse yourself in Scripture itself. Wrestle with it. Question it. Learn from it. And grow from it. Because the word of God brings life and flourishing so that you can enjoy what is best instead of what is merely good (Genesis 1, John 1).

2. Education. Just like a college education requires the pain of about four years of your life for a long-term career, real-life education is one of those things where you experience pain now so you can enjoy pleasure later. Sit down and ask yourself for a moment: who are the people who teach you long-term values? Get around them; spend time with them. Scorning that kind of education to chase pleasure now will lead to pain later. The Bible says in Proverbs 23:23 (ESV), "Buy truth, and do not sell it; buy wisdom, instruction, and understanding." Does this imply truth is for sale? No, it means you must investment time and energy to attain it. The quote may or may not come from Mark Twain, but is more certainly true now than ever before: "A lie travels around the globe while the truth is putting on its shoes." In other words, you're going to have to work to get a hold of truth. Make the investment; it will pay off.

3. Real-life human interaction. Invest in friendships where there is no digital element between you. Put the screen down and make the effort to interact with someone in person. Talk to them face to face. This is especially important while living in a time when the bulk of our interactions are virtual. COVID-19 has unfortunately driven us further from these experiences. An entire generation is growing up with more isolation than ever because of the dramatic levels of detachment our response to this disease has garnered. The science is in from the NIH that stipulates the pain of these policies will hurt many for the long haul. Close relationships decrease inflammation, empowering the immune system to fight off actual disease.[59] My advice is, resist the trend and get in the presence of friends and family whom you love and who love you. Close relationships not only improve your life; they keep your immune system strong!

4. Marriage and family. Whether you're married or single, learn to view marriage and family as a long-term investment. If you were to buy stock and you wanted to get your full investment out of it, you wouldn't jump ship and sell the moment things got a bit shaky. Stocks rise and fall. There are heights and there are dips, and only a dip sells in a dip. The familiar adage suggests we "zoom out" on the stock chart to see that over time, there's always growth. Stop zooming in on the faults in your significant other, and zoom out to the long-term success brought about by faithfulness and integrity. Family is no different. There will be days you say, "My spouse/ kid is the best!" and there will be days you think, "My spouse/ kid is Satan!" But in the long run, the investment will pay out dividends if you don't sell out. (However, keep in mind that it is never worth making a bad investment in a violent abuser. If that is your situation, please seek the help you need to escape that bad investment and find the right people and relationships to invest in.)

Long-Term Living Leans into Admonishment

It is better for a man to hear the rebuke of the wise than to hear the song of fools. For as the crackling of thorns under a pot, so is the laughter of the fools; this also is vanity.
—ECCLESIASTES 7:5–6 (ESV)

In the ancient world, thorns were used as kindling to start a fire, and they would crackle as they burned in the flames. Warren Wiersbe has a great insight to this proverb: if you read this verse in the Hebrew, it's filled with hard K sounds to evoke a phonetic symbolism of those crackling flames in the listener's ear.[60] Having lived in a cold-weather state, I have made my fair share of fires. You always need kindling to get the fire started, but kindling won't make the fire last. In Solomon's time, the common form of kindling was thorns, which made a lot of noise as they burned off quickly.

That is the picture of being scorned, or even applauded, by fools. It arrives quickly but never lasts. Do not give them your attention. On the other hand, hard wood such as oak burns long and slow and produces heat for sustained periods of time. The imagery is striking, and the lesson is powerful when it comes to getting wisdom from those who may correct you. It may not make much noise, but it will lead to long-term prosperity if you pay attention to it.

By contrast, the quick burn of kindling, Solomon says, is like the applause of fools. It's great when someone likes something we do. And it feels good to receive compliments. It can give us a spark of courage to try a new thing. But if we become dependent on those "sparks," we're going to head straight to burn-out. It can be easy to forget that the same people who like or comment on our posts are doing the same thing we do when we're on social media—hitting the heart or thumbs up icon and then scrolling to the next thing, forgetting all about whatever it was they "liked" just a moment before. By the way, have you ever liked or retweeted something you unliked or deleted later, after learning a bit more of the facts? I have, on several occasions. And when I do, it reminds me of how silly our short-term world can get. Wisdom thinks much longer-term.

This is also true in the real world. An uncomfortable truth is this: the people who celebrate you today could be cursing you tomorrow. We see this happening with increasing frequency through the so-called "cancel culture." My wife and I have also experienced this in our own ministry. Early on in our ministry, a family left our church. I remember our closest friend coming up to us that Sunday to assure us they loved us and would never leave. They left two years later. That's life. You either lean into the praise of people or the wisdom of God, which may hurt but is always rooted in love.

Stefani Germanotta is known to the world as Lady Gaga. One of her most popular songs is literally titled, "Applause." The lyrics are not exactly Shakespeare, but they ring true in the hearts of millions seeking fame and celebrity as she confesses to living for people's praise. [61] Three years after that song was released, Netflix produced a special about her. Who could ask for more attention?

Yet, in the special, Stefani admits that all her fame has left her empty. In one scene, she's heard weeping on the phone to her friend: *"I'm alone, Brandon. Every night. And all these people will leave, right? They will leave, and then I'll be alone. And I go from everyone touching me all day and talking at me all day to total silence."* [62]

If you're living for the applause of others, you're going to find that life quickly loses its charm for you. The nature of applause involves one of the quickest sounds the human body can produce—a clap. In half a second, it's over. The empty words will become grating to your ears and bitter in your mouth. You've got to get rid of that appetite now or get a taste for something you may not like initially, but that will bring life to you in the end—rebuke and admonishment from people who are truly invested in your long-term growth.

Who in your life cares about you enough to be honest with you about the things that you don't want to hear about yourself? Proverbs 27:6 (ESV) says, "Faithful are the wounds of a friend; profuse are the kisses of an enemy." With these words, Solomon echoes his father, who says in Psalm 141:5 (ESV), "Let a righteous man strike me—it is a kindness; let him rebuke me—it is oil for my head; let my head not refuse it. Yet my prayer is continually against their evil deeds."

And in Proverbs 12:1 (ESV), Solomon also writes, "Whoever loves discipline loves knowledge, but he who hates reproof is stupid."

We live in a world that increasingly goes out of its way to train us only to listen to others who agree with us. We see it in how we interact with people on social media. We see it in how one news agency pits itself (and its followers) against a rival news agency (and their followers). We see it among our leaders who pit members of one party against members of the opposite party. Some call it an "echo chamber," bouncing our ideas back on ourselves because we only interact with those in agreement. And woe to the person who dares challenge you (or your side) on what you have been trained to believe about matters of this world!

Do you see how unhealthy this is? We are cultivating an entire generation to never listen to anybody outside of their "group." And then we wonder why our lives fail to move forward. We've rejected sincere instruction and rebuke for temporary and undependable applause. Listen, we all need someone who loves us enough to come alongside us from time to time, whack us upside the head, and say, "What are you doing? Stop being a fool."

If you're exhausting yourself by constantly looking for new ways to appeal to your "followers," it's time for a shift in your thinking. Instead of researching the latest way to hack the almighty algorithms, you need to learn how to have stability in the person

God is making you to be—and who you are becoming long-term. Instead of worrying about whether people are saying good things about you today (Ecclesiastes 7:21), you need learn how to stand in your everlasting identity in Christ. Because once you do, you'll find that most of the opinions of others are merely thorns crackling in a fire.

Long-Term Living Looks Forward with Patience

Surely oppression drives the wise into madness, and a bribe corrupts the heart. Better is the end of a thing than its beginning, and the patient in spirit is better than the proud in spirit. Be not quick in your spirit to become angry, for anger lodges in the heart of fools.
—ECCLESIASTES 7:7–9 (ESV)

God has a long-term view of you, and He's not finished with you yet. If you're reading this and thinking, "If you only knew about me what I know about me, you wouldn't be saying that God's got a place in His kingdom for me," then Lamentations 3:22–23 (ESV) has a promise for you: "The steadfast love of the LORD never ceases; his mercies never come to an end; they are new every morning; great is your faithfulness."

God knows you're going to blow it the same way He knows I'm going to blow it. And He accounts for our all failures—especially the spectacularly epic ones—in His daily renewing mercies. When you are in Christ, your indiscretions and failings are not proclaimed against you from the throne of the King. But He will use them to develop you in the long-term.

Solomon talks about shortcuts, events and choices that short-circuit your long-term reality, in Ecclesiastes 7:7–9 (take another look if you glossed over them at the top of this section).

The word "oppression" here is translated "extortion" in the New International Version.[63] Beware of cheating and bribes, anger, and pride. Solomon is talking about the shortcuts life may offer that result in short-term good but long-term pain. That path will only leave you empty.

God is big on small and slow beginnings that reap eternal satisfaction. It took seventy-five years before God called Abraham into the promised land (and longer for him to have a son). It took eighty years before He called Moses to deliver the Israelites. David was running around, dodging Saul's spears and hiding from the king's army, for thirteen years before he was placed on the throne. And God put His own Son in the middle of a small town in nowheresville for thirty years before Jesus ever spoke in public.

God is big on small and slow beginnings because in those small and slow beginnings, you are being formed for long-term successes. Zechariah 4:10 (NLT) says, "Do not despise these small beginnings, for the LORD rejoices to see the work begin." But as you're growing, "say not, 'Why were the former days better than these?' For it is not from wisdom that you ask this" (Ecclesiastes 7:10 ESV).

It's not good to spend your life looking backwards, wishing that things now could be like what they once were. Warren Wiersbe once wrote, "'The good old days' are the combination of a bad memory and a good imagination."[64] If things were good and simple for you at one point but are hard and challenging now, praise the Lord! It could very well be that who you were five years ago wasn't strong enough or mature enough to endure whatever it is that God is beginning to walk you through in this difficult season you currently find yourself in. If He had dropped you into this season back then, it could have destroyed you. Instead, He cared for you enough that He started working in slow, small ways back then to prepare you for such a time as this.

Long-Term Living Acknowledges God Has Control

Consider the work of God: who can make straight what he has made crooked? In the day of prosperity be joyful, and in the day of adversity consider: God has made the one as well as the other, so that man may not find out anything that will be after him.
—ECCLESIASTES 7:13–14 (ESV)

Some of us think a good day means that God is really close to us, and a bad day is when God is the furthest from us. But Scripture actually says the opposite is true. He's near the broken-hearted (Psalm 34:18). Pain, not pleasure, is typically when we lean into God's voice in life. Thus, Solomon asks us to think far more deeply on "the day of adversity." God has something to say. To quote C. S. Lewis directly on this: "God whispers to us in our pleasures, speaks to us in our conscience, but shouts in our pains It is His megaphone to rouse a deaf world."[65] Your present pain or trouble does not mean God has given up on you. It actually means the opposite, and wisdom for the long-term understands this. Scripture says God will *never* leave us or forsake us (Hebrews 13:5).

Long-Term Living Finds "Right Standing" with God

In my vain life I have seen everything. There is a righteous man who perishes in his righteousness, and there is a wicked man who prolongs his life in his evildoing. Be not overly righteous, and do not make yourself too wise. Why should you destroy yourself? Be not overly wicked, neither be a fool. Why should you die before your time?
—ECCLESIASTES 7:15–17 (ESV)

Reread that verse again, because you may be shocked by Solomon's admonition to not be "overly righteous." Aren't we supposed to seek righteousness as much as we can? Yes. But the righteousness that Solomon speaks of in these verses is a bombastic, self-absorbed righteousness rooted in whatever religious works you can perform to make yourself look good. In other words, you believe it's your actions that make you righteous. You and I would call it self-righteousness, which can actually keep you *from* God because you think that you can handle everything on your own by following a list of rules. This was the problem with the Pharisees, scribes, and legal experts in Jesus' day. They knew the Bible very well, but when the Son of God appeared, they rejected Him. Why? Because He testified to their true status before God: that of sinners, not self-made righteous saints. This infuriated them and caused them to miss the grace and salvation Jesus offered them.

True righteousness means that you are in *right standing* with God. It's a judicial term of determination. It means that when God looks at your life, He says, "You're good with Me."

We all want to be good with somebody in the eternal quest for righteousness. The reason why we put makeup on and our best clothes on before we go out of the house is because we want to look good in the eyes of others. The reason why we fudge on our resume and exaggerate in interviews is because we want to look good in the eyes of the employer. The whole of human life is this quest to be good in the eyes of those whose opinions we have set up to really matter. However, if that's our sole aim, we will never feel secure.

There's only one opinion that matters in the long-term. That's God's. And unless you are perfect, you're not good (Ecclesiastes 7:20). But here's the good news: the true Son of Solomon, the descendent of King David, was perfect. He never sinned. He was morally blameless and faultless. And we took that perfect man and put Him on a cross. But on that cross, two thousand years ago, the righteous man perished in His righteousness so that the evil man—you and me—could live long lives *in spite of our evil.*

First Corinthians 1:30 (ESV) says, "And because of him you are in Christ Jesus, who became to us wisdom from God, righteousness and sanctification and redemption."

That's the gospel, my friend! No one's getting to heaven based on what they do. Everyone who is getting into heaven is getting there based on what Jesus did for them—*for you.* If you want to experience the joys of living a long-term life, this is it. This is God's long-term plan for anyone born in this short-term world.

WORKBOOK

llllllllllllllllllllllllllllllllll

Chapter Four Questions

Question: What is the difference between wisdom and knowledge? Do you think your life is characterized by the pursuit of wisdom? How do you know? Describe an experience God used in your life to grow you in wisdom.

_____

_____

_____

_____

_____

_____

_____

_____

_____

_____

Question: What do you observe yourself looking for when you feel restless, to bring your heart reprieve? What is the result of pursing, consuming, or engaging with those things? Do you think there is a better way to cope with a restless heart? If so, what do you think that is? How can you more intentionally pursue that option?

_____

_____

_____

_____

_____

_____

_____

_____

_____

_____

_____

_____

Journal: What aspects of long-term living are evident in your life? For each category of long-term living (long-term living seeks to make investments; long-term living leans into admonishment; long-term living looks forward with patience; long-term living acknowledges God has control; long-term living finds "right standing" with God), journal about how you see this reflected in your life. Then follow it with how you need to grow in that area.

_____

_____

_____

_____

_____

_____

_____

_____

_____

_____

Action: Read Ecclesiastes 7:1–14. As you read through it, underline or highlight every instance of the word **better** that you come across. Think about all the good things you've wanted at one point in time or another throughout your life. How many times did you get that good thing and think it's not that great? Now think about a time you didn't get that good thing but eventually ended up with something **better** down the road. Maybe it was something you would have missed out on altogether had you gotten that **good thing** right when you wanted it. Examine this list whenever you find yourself in a situation when you need to trust God for the **better thing** in your life.

_____

_____

_____

_____

_____

_____

_____

_____

_____

_____

_____

Chapter Four Notes

‖‖‖

_____

_____

_____

_____

_____

_____

_____

_____

_____

_____

_____

_____

_____

_____

_____

_____

_____

_____

_____

_____

_____

_____

_____

‖‖

Finding Joy in the Midst of Unpleasant Realities

Who is like the wise? And who knows the interpretation of a thing? A man's
wisdom makes his face shine, and the hardness of his face is changed.
—ECCLESIASTES 8:1 (ESV)

othing can make life feel empty faster than the unfair challenges people face, the injustice we see or experience ourselves,
and the ways in which we often watch the good guy get what
the bad guy deserves. So when we turn to Ecclesiastes 8, we find
ourselves in good company with our mentor Solomon for finding
meaning in the seemingly meaningless results inevitable to life. The
key word in verse 1? *Interpretation.* The word here in Hebrew means
"clarification of the meaning or significance of something." [66] Life
is filled with joy-sucking realities. If you're not careful, you'll let it
drain your joy. But do not despair! Wisdom is available to help you
understand it from a healthy biblical mindset.

If you're living in the same world I'm living in, you're going to
face innumerable hardships. You're also going to witness things
going on around you that may depress your spirit and rob your

89

life of joy. But godly wisdom, Solomon says in the opening line of Ecclesiastes 8, brings peace to a disquieted soul and resurrects a dying spirit.

Why does he start this way? Because in chapters 8 and 9, he's going to unwrap some uncomfortable truths and unpleasant realities of life. The funny thing is, he talked about things going on in the world almost three thousand years ago and they're still as true as if he wrote them today.

Human understanding focuses on all the problems and trying to find solutions that we ourselves can bring to them. But too often, these problems are far too big for us to handle, so we become discouraged and disgruntled. However, Solomon encourages us, if we get hold of what God reveals and if we sink our lives into what He wants for us, it's going to make us healthy and happy.

WISDOM MAKES YOU HEALTHY AND HAPPY

We spend an increasing amount of time discussing how our mental state impacts our well-being, but are you aware that your spiritual state affects your physical body as well?[67] The research has been done about this again and again, proving that people with a heart aligned with the gospel live healthier and happier lives overall.

A report published by U. K.-based Christian Medical Fellowship says that "those who have faith carry positive health benefits such as coping with illness, faster recovery, as well as protection from future illnesses." It also concludes that "people with mental health problems, such as psychosis, also proved to cope better when religion was involved." [68]

Even some studies that weren't Christian-based have found that faith and religion play a part in health, stating that "regular service attendance was linked to reductions in the body's stress responses and even in mortality—so much so that worshippers were 55%

less likely to die during the up to 18-year follow-up period than people who didn't frequent the temple, church or mosque."[69]

We must speak to our spirits about the truth of God's word so that the reality of what God has done for us in Christ roots itself in our hearts. Only then will our spirits be alive with the truth of the resurrection. When we speak to our spirits with God's word, it brings life. It brings joy. And then it radiates out into the physical reality of our existence.

In the last two chapters, I outlined a few benefits of having God's wisdom in our lives. I'm going to quickly sum up the first two again and then introduce the third thing wisdom teaches us, because we need to be regularly reminded of the importance of having wisdom.

1. Wisdom **separates** *God's best from what seems good* (Proverbs 14:12; Proverbs 16:25). Life will present options that look, feel, or seem right to you. Wisdom says, "Wait. Pause. Maybe what looks right isn't right." Our judgment and understanding are limited, but God knows the end from the beginning and wants to spare us from outcomes we can't foresee.

2. Wisdom **prepares** *us to choose the hard road instead of the easy escape* (Proverbs 12:1, Hebrews 12:11). Satan tempts us with pleasure now and blinds us to the pain that will inevitably come later. Wisdom says, "It's hard to say no to that temptation now, but the benefits of waiting for the pleasure that comes in God's time will be more than worth it."

3. Wisdom **grounds** *us in reality instead of fantasy.* Christianity is not about escapism. It's not about getting out of here to get to someplace better. We should care about our world. We should care about people. We should care about the

things around us. This is biblical wisdom that grounds us in reality.

While it might not always feel like it, the world that God created is good, not evil. The whole of Scripture shows us that God is working to restore creation to its intended state and to make all things new.

Unfortunately, there is a tendency in Christianity to become "super-spiritual." When our focus becomes hyper-fixated on the spiritual, we can see demons everywhere. Instead of a flat tire on the way to work being the result of running over a nail, we see it as the work of the devil, whose sole purpose was to make us late for an important meeting and to put us into a foul mood for the rest of the day.

Yes, there is a spiritual realm, and yes there are evil spirits at work in our world (Ephesians 6:12), but not everything we come up against in life is a spiritual battle. Sometimes a nail is just a nail. Biblical wisdom helps us recognize what is spiritual and what is physical, and how to deal with both.

LIFE IS CHALLENGING AND CONFUSING

Many are the plans in the mind of a man, but it is the purpose of the
Lord that will stand.
—PROVERBS 19:21 (ESV)

Here's the thing: we all make plans—and then reality happens. You plan to retire at the age of fifty-five, but what happens if the company you work for exports your job when you're forty-five? You plan to be married by the time you're thirty. But what happens if you don't meet somebody before then? You think, "I'm going to squeeze every pleasurable moment I can out of life before I give my life over to Jesus!" But what if one of those fun nights ends your life?

We make plans. Then reality happens.

There are three realities that Solomon expounds on in Ecclesiastes 8 and 9.

1. *The first reality he points out to us is this: life is unpredictable.*

> *Indeed, how can people avoid what they don't know is going to happen? None of us can hold back our spirit from departing. None of us has the power to prevent the day of our death. There is no escaping that obligation, that dark battle. And in the face of death, wickedness will certainly not rescue the wicked.*
> —ECCLESIASTES 8:7–8 (NLT)

God is up to something that you're not fully aware of, so things are not going always to go according to your plans and expectations. There will be people who try to promise you the world, who will tell you something is a "sure thing," but I'm telling you that anyone who promises you the good life in "six easy steps" or "nine easy payments" is selling you something. And it isn't anything you want.

This is the harsh reality of our life: you buy a hot stock and it tanks. You buy your first house and there are serious problems with the foundation or heating system. You get a dream job only to discover the corporation is steeped in corruption (see the movie *Fun with Dick and Jane* [70]). You plan a future life with someone, but then the relationship ends. You chat with a friend one day, and the next day you learn they're gone.

If you're banking on these things to bring you contentment, you'll once again sink into a sense of emptiness. Make plans, dream dreams, and take risks, but hold all of these loosely, because life is unpredictable and only God knows what's truly coming next.

2. *The second thing that Solomon points out to us in verses 9 and 10 (NLT) is that life is unjust.*

> I have thought deeply about all that goes on here under the sun, where people have the power to hurt each other. I have seen wicked people buried with honor. Yet they were the very ones who frequented the Temple and are now praises in the same city where they committed their crimes! This, too, is meaningless. When a crime is not punished quickly, people feel it is safe to do wrong.

If ever there were a text that applies to our modern life, it is this one. The world was thrown into anger, confusion, and division following the death of George Floyd[71] and the unrelenting politicization of that tragic day. There seems to be an inordinate desire to be soft on crime, which leads to more crime as a result. As I write this, New York City mourns the murder of two Hispanic police officers at the hands of a criminal who was released on probation.[72] It seems that we swing from one extreme to the other in trying to get justice right.

Here's the truth: we won't get it fully right, because we are constantly favoring ourselves, our people, or even our ethnicity. This is the tragic nature of sin in the human condition, and something Solomon wrestled with greatly.

One of my favorite musicals is *The Sound of Music*,[73] and no, I'm not ashamed to admit it. After the handsome and wealthy Captain Von Trapp professes his love to Maria, she breaks out into song: "Nothing comes from nothing. Nothing ever could. But somewhere in my youth or childhood, I must have done something good." [74]

See the tendency? She was receiving something good, because she must have done something good. I find this sort of imagination even among Christians. Good things happen to us when we are good people who do good things. News flash! That's not even close to Christianity. That's Hinduism. And there are more American Christians going about life living this blend of Hindu-Christianity than any of us might care to admit. If this is your approach, then of course you will be filled with a sense of hopeless dread when you're "doing everything right" and yet keep discovering that life is hard and unpredictable. Sometimes you do all the rights things but things still turn out badly for you. And sometimes you do what's bad, yet you get what's good.

In 2019, after American troops targeted and killed ISIS leader al-Baghdadi, one of our American newspapers wrote an obituary describing how the "austere religious scholar al-Baghdadi" had died at age forty-eight.[75] This man was evil. He was a terrorist who was responsible for horrific acts of violence throughout the Middle East, but in that instance, he was painted in a golden light.

We live in a world that wants to deny that evil exists. We twist and repackage our words so that evil men who take the lives of the innocent through violence while following their religious convictions—even to death—are painted as good, while those whose religious convictions lead them to fight within the legal system to preserve the lives of the innocent are painted as evil.

Don't mistake me here. There have been bad leaders in the Christian church as well. Leaders in the Christian movement have hurt and abused children. They have caused irreparable mental, emotional, and physical harm to the very people they are called to protect. Jesus had some very choice words for these people, and for those of us who turn a blind eye to their actions. He once said, "Whoever causes one of these little ones who believe in me to sin, it would be better for him if a great millstone were hung around his neck and he were thrown into the sea" (Mark 9:42 ESV). Jesus has little patience for evil leaders.

Solomon tells us that sometimes the bad guys get what the good guys deserve (life) and the good guys get what the bad guys deserve (death). And after almost three thousand years, we still haven't figured out that "when a crime is not punished quickly, people feel it is safe to do wrong" (Ecclesiastes 8:11 NLT).

We live in a society where people are anxious to do away with the death penalty for murderers, yet this same society has no qualms about murdering an unborn child who has committed no wrong. Some might say I'm getting too political here, but I'm not being political. I'm being ethical and biblical. The more we turn these ethical issues into political debates, the more it corrupts our society and sickens our hearts.

3. The final point that Solomon makes about life is that it's often unfair. In verse 14, he says, "And this is not all that is meaningless in our world. In this life, good people are often treated as though they were wicked, and wicked people are often treated as though they were good. This is so meaningless!" (NLT).

Leaders like Abraham Lincoln and Martin Luthor King, Jr., are examples of men who were cut down unjustly while fighting for justice. Yet, dictators like Stalin, who was responsible for the mass murder of millions of his own people, live until their natural death from old age. This is just unjust and unfair.

You only have to spend three days on this earth to realize life isn't fair. Just ask any kid, including mine. In fact, it's a favorite thing to complain about even after we grow up. We complain about the unfair treatment we receive in the workforce, in the home, in the education system, etc. We just have a different word for it as we get older: in today's society, it's called inequality. And while there is a certain truth to this, there is a shadow mission hidden beneath all that noise—whether its pertaining to heterosexual and homosexual relationships, gender equality, racial equality, or any other form of equality that society is demanding. Now let me shock your sensibilities: equality isn't a biblical ideal. God does not give equal portions to human beings or families. Take a look at the Parable of the Talents in Matthew 25:14–30 for just one example. Equality is a worldly mantra, and many countries have devastated their economies trying to make all things equal. You would think we'd have learned this lesson after seventy years of communism in the Soviet Union destroyed their economy, or the devastation socialism caused to a once-great economic powerhouse in Venezuela. The truth is, a basic understanding of life embraces some measure of inequality no matter who we are. A youngest child in the family typically is afforded the benefits of his or her parent's firmer financial standing than the first-born. This is not injustice; it's life.

Some people get a lucky break. Some people don't. Some people miraculously recover from sickness. Some people don't. Why? Because life isn't fair and none of us receives equal treatment. Does this mean we don't work toward making things more equitable for those around us? No. It does mean that we stop looking at inequality itself as a stop sign in life. Many people have risen from poverty to prosperity, defied the odds, and overcome diverse obstacles to accomplish great things. They did this by ignoring the inequities and embracing their opportunities.

SUCCESS IS A LOT OF
RIGHT PLACE/RIGHT TIME

Again I saw that under the sun the race is not to the swift, nor the battle to the strong, nor bread to the wise, nor riches to the intelligent, nor favor to those with knowledge, but time and chance happen to them all.
—ECCLESIASTES 9:11 (ESV)

Malcom Gladwell talks about the story of Bill Gates in his book *Outliers*, [76] and in the second chapter, he discusses how, many times as a kid, Bill happened to be in the right place at the right time to go on to become one of the richest and most recognized men of our time.

When Bill was in eighth grade, his mother was part of a mom's group that held a bake sale every year to buy something for his class with the proceeds. In 1965, the bake sale was so successful, they bought a PC for the students. Bill fell in love with computing because of that computer, but so did everyone else in that class. Back in those days, getting the computer to perform any function required punching holes in a card, then putting the card in the computer to "read." Gates was consumed and challenged by the process, and he kept with it until he couldn't go any further.

It so happens that the University of Washington was conveniently across the street from his high school, and they happened to have one of the *few* next level computers he needed to improve his computing skills. And it just so happened that he met a guy there named Paul Allen who would become his friend first and his partner four years later.

Right place. Right time.

We can do all the right things, put in all the long hours, and never see that big break. Why? Because life is unpredictable, unjust, and unfair. The question put to us by Solomon is this: "What are we going to do with that knowledge?"

Are we going to freak out? Are we going to blame God or others because we never received our heart's desire? Thank God, Solomon doesn't say, "Well, guys. Here's the thing. Life stinks, and that's just the way it is. God bless." Instead, he walks us through how to face some of the unpleasant realities of life with an unshakeable contentment.

HOW TO FACE UNPLEASANT REALITIES

Though a sinner does evil a hundred times and prolongs his life,
yet I know that it will be well with those who fear God,
because they fear before him.
—ECCLESIASTES 8:12 (ESV)

When we recognize that God is over everything in life and that He's in control, we learn to fear Him. Solomon is not talking about cowering, shaking, and wanting to run and hide from God; he is talking about living a life that honors God and respects His authority as the greatest Being in heaven and on earth, then worships Him for it, specifically in the midst of life's unfairness.

Maintain the Right Fear

Solomon talks about the "fear of God" in this passage because he has learned the importance of putting God and God alone on the pedestal of your life. To fear God is to esteem His opinion above all others.

Here's the thing: we are controlled by the thing we fear most. It's what gets the greatest amount of our attention. If our fear is finances, then money (the lack or abundance of it) dictates how we make every major decision in life. Money is what we think about on our way to work and on our way home. Disagreements over the finances in our home will wreck our marriage and hurt our relationship with our family. All because we fear not having enough and we have made money "god."

If our fear is the opinion of others, we live in fear of letting our friends and family down. We worry about where we stand with acquaintances and co-workers who aren't even truly invested in our life, and we're letting them call the shots about who we're going to be.

Fearing and giving reverence to people and things leads to a life filled with misery and uncertainty; it robs of you of the best life God intends for you. But when you fear God and you make Him the chief focus of your life, you begin to recognize the value and the purpose He created in your life and your reason for being here on this earth. Not to serve yourself and the unfulfilling wants and desires that have no lasting value, but to serve the One who set aside His own life so that you could experience a full and abundant life (John 10:10).

When life gets difficult, remember you live under the sovereignty of God.

Maintain an Underserving Attitude

Every song, commercial, and worldly mantra programs us to think we "deserve" something. Social media parading the best parts of others' lives across our screens teaches us to envy others. Without us being actively aware of it, these outside forces are shaping our characters and mindsets.

Solomon's answer to the emptiness of entitlement is maintaining an undeserving attitude. When you look around your life and see all that is good, do you say, "God, I didn't deserve that. It's a gift from You"?

What are the blessings you see coming from your relationship with your spouse? Are you thanking God for them? If you have kids and they're healthy and alive, do you thank Him for that blessing? You may have a job you dislike, but thank God for providing for you financially. You may not have the trendiest wardrobe, but thank God for the clothes on your back.

The apostle James wrote, "Every good gift and every perfect gift is from above, coming down from the Father of lights, with whom there is no variation or shadow due to change" (James 1:17 ESV). God is good to you.

Solomon also guides us through some choices we should make when we're maintaining this underserving attitude. Choose joyful ventures in your life (Ecclesiastes 8:15) so that the unpleasant things don't dominate your life. That might mean putting down the news and picking up a good fiction book or getting outside and going for a hike.

Choose to enjoy your loved ones (Ecclesiastes 9:9). Spend quality time with the people you love instead of zoning out on your phone or the latest streaming app. Research has shown that love grows toward someone the more time you spend with them.[77] Are you feeling distant from your spouse? Spend time with him or her! Do you feel like you aren't connecting with your kids? Engage in an activity you all enjoy that requires that you look at each other and interact with each other.

Choose to enjoy your work (Ecclesiastes 9:10). It's been said, "It's not by searching for special things that we find joy, but by making the everyday things special." The job you have now may very well be preparing you for a job you aren't expecting later on. But even if that's not the case for you, look for opportunities to excel at it, anyway. And thank God for the position He's placed you in *at this time.*

Remember the Unseen Victory of Jesus

I have also seen this example of wisdom under the sun, and it seemed great to me. There was a little city with few men in it, and a great king came against it and besieged it, building great siegeworks against it. But there was found in it a poor, wise man, and he by his wisdom delivered the city. Yet no one remembered that poor man. But I say that wisdom is better than might, though the poor man's wisdom is despised and his words are not heard.
—ECCLESIASTES 9:13–16 (ESV)

Solomon has seen it all. He has observed all of life—the good and the bad—and he sums it all up with a story of a poor, wise man who delivered a great city from a formidable king, only to be forgotten by the people he saved.

When I look at this story, I see a man who faced an unjust, unpredictable, and unfair situation. He lived in a small, inconsequential town. Who could have predicted a great and powerful king would bring his entire army against it? And where was the justice in that one, small man risking his life and saving the city, only to be forgotten?

When I look at this story, I see Jesus all over it. Jesus faced unfairness. Second Corinthians 8:9 tells us that for our sake, He became poor so that we, by His poverty, might become rich. Jesus faced the unpredictable. Matthew 27:1–2 shows the leading priests and elders—the very men who should have recognized and welcomed Christ as the Messiah they'd been waiting for—laying plans to put Jesus to death under Roman law. And Jesus bore injustice. Again, in 2 Corinthians 5:21, we read that Jesus, who never sinned, took on our sin so that we might take on His righteousness before God.

Unfair. Unpredictable. Unjust.

But Jesus won. Colossians 2:15 says that Jesus "disarmed the spiritual rulers and authorities. He shamed them publicly by his victory over them on the cross" (NLT). How? By submitting Himself to injustice and unfairness at the highest degree.

He knew what we need to be aware of each and every day: the real enemies of your life are the devil, hell, and sin. Unfortunately, like that poor man in Solomon's story, His sacrifice has been forgotten by many. And because they have forgotten, they are living in misery. Solomon shared this story to remind us that life is unfair, but we serve a God who is above it all.

When unfairness gets you bitter, when injustice gets you disbelieving in God, and when what you didn't expect happens and you want to quit, get back to Jesus. He's been there. He's suffered with you. And He won the unseen battle for you.

When the outside of your life looks defeated, remember the victory of Christ for your eternity is completed. You can face the unpleasant realities of life with eternal hope in your heart.

WORKBOOK

||||||||||||||||||||||||||||||||||||

Chapter Five Questions

Question: Look at the list of what wisdom does (it separates God's best from what seems good; it prepares us to choose the hard road instead of the easy escape; it grounds us in reality instead of fantasy). Do you see evidence of these functions of wisdom in your life? Which do you see the most of? Which do you see the least of? What changes do you need to pursue to allow God's wisdom to have more power in your life?

_____

_____

_____

_____

_____

_____

_____

_____

_____

_____

_____

_____

Question: How does knowing that life is often unpredictable, unjust, and unfair—regardless of the kind of person you are or how you live—affect your expectations for and perspective on your life circumstances?

_____

_____

_____

_____

_____

_____

_____

_____

_____

_____

_____

_____

Journal: No matter what you are going through right now, journal a prayer of praise and thanksgiving to God for who He is.

_____

_____

_____

_____

_____

_____

_____

_____

_____

_____

_____

Action: Shift your perspective by counting your blessings. In a notebook or journal, begin the practice of documenting in writing all the things you have to be thankful for—including salvation through Christ.

_____

_____

_____

_____

_____

_____

_____

_____

_____

_____

_____

_____

Chapter Five Notes

||||||||||||||||||||||||||||||||||||||||||||||||||||||||||||

_____

_____

_____

_____

_____

_____

_____

_____

_____

_____

_____

_____

_____

_____

_____

_____

_____

_____

_____

_____

_____

_____

_____

CHAPTER SIX

||||||||||||||||||||||||||||||||||||||||||

The Gospel's Answer to Difficult People

Wisdom is better than weapons of war,
but one sinner destroys much good.
—ECCLESIASTES 9:18 (ESV)

When Solomon surveys the wisdom needed to answer life's emptiness, he spends a bunch of time on something we've all experienced one way or another: difficult people. It may not be readily apparent, but a difficult relationship can cap our emotional energy and positive spirit quickly—leading us to question, *"What's the point?"*

We've all been there. You finally get that job you wanted and you're going to start your life's work. At first, things seem so new and exciting. Then *they* show up. They were there before, but you didn't notice them. Then you have that one awkward conversation that will lead to hurt feelings and frustration for weeks, months, years, or decades.

Or you finally got into that college. You move into the dorms. You meet new people. Life is full of excitement for what's to come. Then you meet that *one* professor who it seems is out to get you.

Or you got married, you went on the honeymoon, and you had the time of your life. Then you came home and realized you married a difficult person. Now the things that seemed so cute and innocent while you were dating are anything but.

ONE PERSON CAN HAVE THE POWER TO MAKE LIFE STINK

Dead flies make the perfumer's ointment give off a stench; so a little folly outweighs wisdom and honor.
—ECCLESIASTES 10:1 (ESV)

Here are three hard facts about difficult people: they are everywhere, they can affect anyone, and they may not know that they are difficult. The truth is, we are often looking to our relationships to satisfy and fulfill us. When we are putting our hope in others and then are continually met with their difficult attributes, it can lead us to a sense of insecurity and emptiness.

The reason why there are difficult people everywhere is because of sin. Human beings are sinners. Before they have nationalities, colors, creeds, or genders, they are sinners. And sin brings disharmony into our relationships. I wrote about this concept back in Chapter Two. Sin doesn't just separate us from God—who in His very nature is a perfect, harmonious community of Father, Son, and Holy Spirit—but it also separates us from each other.

Ecclesiastes 7:20 (ESV) says, "Surely there is not a righteous man on earth who does good and never sins." We are people who fall short of the glory of God. We aren't good by nature. Therefore, our world is going to be filled with challenging relationships.

Solomon spends Ecclesiastes 10 talking about how many times he had to deal with difficult people! Now, it took me a while to see this. But who would a king have a difficult relationship with? Another *king*. If a king had a difficult subordinate—in the ancient world, especially—the difficult subordinate didn't have a head much longer. But it's a little trickier when dealing with another head of state. In Ecclesiastes 10:5–7 (ESV), we read:

> There is an evil that I have seen under the sun, as it were an error proceeding from the ruler: folly is set in many high places, and the rich sit in a low place. I have seen slaves on horses, and princes walking on the ground like slaves.

Solomon says some people are in positions of power who should not be there because they live foolishly. Bosses and business owners can have difficult vendors or treacherous competitors. Presidents can have difficult legislators and bitter relationships with other world leaders. Governors can have difficult state houses. Pastors can have difficult parishioners. Things become tense and disharmonious, and if they're not careful and don't find a way to deal with those difficult people, it can lead to disaster.

Here's something to remember about difficult people: some people go out of their way to be difficult, but most difficult people probably don't know they are being difficult. This is what Solomon means when he say, "Even when the fool walks on the road, he lacks sense, and he says to everyone that he is a fool" (Ecclesiastes 10:3 ESV). The text implies that the only one who doesn't know he's a fool *is the fool*. They just don't know. And let's be honest, sometimes that fool—that difficult person—is you.

Everyone is a sinner. Everyone has flaws. Everyone has issues that are going to rub other people the wrong way. And there are people you've come across in life who are bothered by something about you, but you just don't realize it. Or maybe you sense that something is off between you and that someone, but you can't put a finger on what that something is. So you try harder to smooth things over with them, but it only seems to make things worse.

No matter how hard you try, you can't be besties with everyone. Abraham and Lot's servants quarreled over land allotments, so the uncle and nephew parted ways (Genesis 13:5–8). Paul and Barnabas quarreled about whether John Mark should be allowed to go with them on their second missionary journey after he had ditched them during the first one (Acts 15:36–41). Brothers James and John ended up in hot water with the other disciples after their mom asked Jesus to elevate them to his left and right hand (Matthew 20:20–28). We need companionship and community, but those things can't and won't be our ultimate source of fulfilment.

DON'T RUN AWAY FROM DIFFICULT PEOPLE

If the anger of the ruler rises against you, do not leave your place, for calmness will lay great offenses to rest.
—ECCLESIASTES 10:4 (ESV)

Do yourself a favor and underline *"Do not leave your place"* in your Bible. It's just a fact of life that sometimes you are in a challenging relationship with someone and you shouldn't leave. Solomon talks about this in Ecclesiastes 8:2–6 (NLT) as well, when he says:

Obey the king since you vowed to God that you would. Don't try to avoid doing your duty, and don't stand with those who plot evil, for the king can do whatever he wants. His command is backed by great power. No one can resist or question it. Those who obey him will not be punished. Those who are wise will find a time and a way to do what is right, for there is a time and a way for everything, even when a person is in trouble.

Before we go any further, I want to make it clear that we're talking about *difficult* people here, not *abusive* people. There's a difference, and you should run away from abusive people. If you are in an abusive relationship, get out. If you're in a job where there is abuse going on behind closed doors, get out. But, Solomon says, when it comes to dealing with difficult people, don't freak out!

Stop trying to run away from something just because it's hard. Make life easier by avoiding gossip and circular conversations that will only make you feel more trapped and more resentful. And be patient. You don't know how God is going to walk you through to the other side yet.

There's also another scenario to keep in mind. Sometimes you'll find yourself in a challenging relationship with someone and you cannot leave. Maybe the job market is too tight and there's not another job that's easy to come by, so you have to put up with that lazy co-worker who keeps shifting all their work over to you. Maybe you enrolled in a program and have a classmate or professor who's making life miserable for you, but you have a future to think about. Maybe your spouse is paying attention to the needs of everyone and everything except yours, but your kids need a mother and a father in the home.

Solomon says, "Don't freak out. Stick it out." Here's why: that difficult person will show up again. What I mean is, that "character" will show up again. If you move, or relocate, or quit and get a new job, that person who bugs you right now will be at the new place waiting for you. Different skin, same spirit. Different name, same nastiness. Different accent, same attitude.

If all you ever do is run away from difficult people, you won't develop into the fullness of character that God intends for you.

Let Difficult People Develop You

He who digs a pit will fall into it, and a serpent will bite him who breaks
through a wall. He who quarries stones is hurt by them, and he who
splits logs is endangered by them. If the iron is blunt, and one does
not sharpen the edge, he must use more strength, but wisdom helps
one to succeed. If the serpent bites before it is charmed, there is no
advantage to the charmer.
—ECCLESIASTES 10:8–11 (ESV)

I'd like you to stop and picture that difficult person in your life
for a moment. What is it that makes the person difficult to work
with, relate to, or get along with? Now I want you to picture him
or her as a God's University class assignment. It's a basic require-
ment for God's University program of life—meaning, you cannot
graduate until you pass. Sorry. It's not an elective. If you run away
from the difficult person, it's like dropping out of the class. You
get a DO (Dropped Out) on the report card, and you're not off
the hook.

God is the kind of academic dean who doesn't give up on a
single student. When you drop out of a difficult relationship, God
says, "No problem. I've enrolled you again for the next semester
so that you will be molded and shaped into the person that I want
you to be. You keep running away because you don't think they're
good for you, but I say otherwise."

God doesn't give up on you. He assigns you projects (and
people) that irritate you for a reason: personal development. And
the first thing we must learn is how to shift our mindset about
how we respond to the difficult people in our lives. Lori Gottlieb,
a psychotherapist, wrote in an op-ed in the *New York Times* that
she sees fewer and fewer patients who recognize the need for a

change in themselves, and more and more patients who are simply interested in complaining about everyone else.[78]

Twenty years ago, we went to a psychotherapist because we recognized that there was something about ourselves that needed help or mending. Now we're paying someone else hundreds of dollars an hour just to tell them that everyone in the world *but us* needs to change.

Do you realize how powerless that makes you? If everyone around you is truly responsible for everything that's hard in your life, and if there is absolutely nothing you can do to change a thing about it, you're going to be trapped in an endless cycle of anger, hostility, and misery.

We can't change others—their behaviors, their thought patterns, their annoying quirks, any of it. The only one we can do anything about is ourselves. And God's advice for people with difficult relationships is this: start with changing you!

Let Difficult People Teach You to Trust God's Timing

He who digs a pit will fall into it, and a serpent will bite
him who breaks through a wall.
—ECCLESIASTES 10:8 (ESV)

Digging a pit is an act of animus or treachery. David was no stranger to living a life where someone was out to get him. In Psalm 35:7 (ESV), he says, "For without cause they hid their net for me; without cause they dug a pit for my life." There was seldom a time when there wasn't an attack on his life or on his character— beginning with his father and brothers, who didn't think he was worth calling in from the fields when they were visited by Samuel (1 Samuel 16), and ending with one of his own sons, who chased him out of his palace and tried to claim his throne toward the end of his life (2 Samuel 15). The thing that got David through was the trust he'd learned to place in God.

Breaking through a wall is also an act of attack. In the days of walled cities, the primary aim of an attacking army was to destroy the protective barriers surrounding the people. They'd come against city walls with everything they had, hoping to break through and take the city by storm, while those trapped inside the city walls had limited options.

Yes, there are people in your life who are digging pits in your life, people who are deliberately trying to sabotage you or ruin your credibility. They want to destroy your name and your peace. But Solomon says, those trying to attack us may get more than they bargained for (Ecclesiastes10:8). God's wisdom in moments when you're dealing with someone who's gunning for you is this: *be patient in the midst of personal attack*, because the person coming against you will either fall into their own trap or get bit by something unexpected along the way. In other words, their character will catch up to them somewhere.

Furthermore, Scripture promises us that God always repays. And He repays right on time, in a way that is so much better than you could ever do. We see proof of this in the book of Esther with a guy named Haman. He hated the Jews because the Jewish man Mordecai wouldn't bow down to him. Haman built gallows to hang Mordecai, but Mordecai didn't back down or run away. He did his job and honored the king. At the right time, the king found out about Mordecai's kindness and elevated him, while Haman's treachery led him straight to the very gallows he had built for Mordecai.

Be patient. Trust that God sees what that difficult person is doing. He knows the struggles you're facing. And He's not only working through this season to develop your character through the struggle, but He's also laying the groundwork to bring about some form of blessing in your life that you would never have thought to ask for.

Let Difficult People Teach You to Develop Wisdom

He who quarries stones is hurt by them, and he who splits logs is endangered by them. If the iron is blunt, and one does not sharpen the edge, he must use more strength.
—ECCLESIASTES 10:9–10 (ESV)

Verse 8 in Ecclesiastes 10 talks about the people in life who have made it their life's mission to destroy you. But verses 9 and 10 show us a different sort of difficult person. They're not maliciously out to get you; they're just clueless.

I like the wording used in the New Living Translation for verse 10. It says, "Using a dull ax requires great strength, so sharpen the blade." In other words, develop wisdom in your response to those who are continually bugging you.

Maybe you need to think about how you choose to respond to that person. If you're constantly complaining about people who act, think, talk, or view life a certain way that bugs you, may I lovingly suggest that it is *you* who needs to learn how to grow up? Sharpen the blade. That person may have been sent into your life to show you an area in your life where you need to be less sensitive and more compassionate toward others. Spiritual maturity is going from hard-hearted and thin-skinned to soft-hearted and thick-skinned.

Solomon writes, "If the serpent bites before it is charmed, there is no advantage to the charmer" (verse 11 ESV). The word for "charmer" here is also the Hebrew word for tongue, language, or speech. Our internal response to a situation results in our external response—the way we speak and treat others who rub us the wrong way. Our natural response is to lash out, to complain, and to fume. But the New Testament tells us to bless those who persecute us (Romans 12:14) and not to repay evil with evil, but with good (Romans 12:17, 1 Peter 3:9).

Before sending them out on their first solo mission, Jesus told His disciples, "Look, I am sending you out as sheep among wolves. So be as shrewd as snakes and harmless as doves" (Matthew 10:16 NLT). I love the fact that Jesus warned us that people will be awful to us, and that our response should be one that shows good judgment. We have to be shrewd in our relationships with others, because sometimes the difficult things we face are a result of spiritual forces (Ephesians 6:12), while other times it's because we're dealing with the natural consequences of living in a fallen world with fallen people.

If you're a new Christian and you're wondering why people are so mean about your new faith, here's why: their heart is not right with God, and you're the closest thing they'll ever get to Him, so a lot of their anger toward God is going to be directed at you. Learn from Jesus.

Some people are just nasty, and it doesn't matter what you say or do; they're just going to go on being nasty. Be careful about the time and space you give them. Matthew 7:6 (ESV) says, "Do not give dogs what is holy, and do not throw your pearls before pigs, lest they trample them underfoot and turn to attack you."

Isn't it amazing that Jesus—this guy whom we have re-imagined as being happy, soft, cuddly, and loving everybody—says that some people are pigs? He realized that some people don't need or deserve your attention. You're not a whipping post. And if you're getting into the same debates with the non-believers in your life, thinking that eventually you're going to wear them down, stop it! You aren't wearing them down. They're wearing you down. Walk away from that discussion and be at peace. Let God deal with them as He wills, in His time.

WATCH WHAT YOU SAY

The words of a wise man's mouth win him favor, but the lips of a fool consume him. The beginning of the words of his mouth is foolishness, and the end of his talk is evil madness. A fool multiplies words, though no man knows what is to be, and who can tell him what will be after him? The toil of a fool wearies him, for he does not know the way to the city. ... Even in your thoughts, do not curse the king.
—ECCLESIASTES 10:12–15, 10:20 (ESV)

In the age of social media, especially, be careful about what you say about difficult people. When that difficult person comes and needles you, you don't have to respond in kind (or at all). Proverbs 15:1 (ESV) says, "A soft answer turns away wrath, but a harsh word stirs up anger."

Before responding to an online dig or a personal attack, ask yourself, "Will responding to this person escalate things? Or will it deescalate tension?" Then act accordingly.

The best advice I can give about when to do when aggravated is, *never write it down.* What I mean by this is, learn when to keep your thoughts to yourself, or if necessary, talk to the person you're involved with personally, face to face (see Matthew 18). Solomon says the same thing in Ecclesiastes 10:20 (ESV):

Even in your thoughts, do not curse the king, nor in your own bedroom curse the rich, for a bird of the air will carry your voice, or some winged creature with tell the matter.

When someone wants to share a rumor, what do they say? "A little bird told me." What's the logo for Twitter? A little bird. *(I realize it has since changed its name to X.)* Those words you type in with your thumbs on your phone and send out to the Twitterverse without considering the weight of them can and will come back to haunt you.

Comedian Gilbert Gottfried was the voice of the Aflac insurance company's "duck" for several years. In 2011 he showed poor judgment in a tweet about a tsunami that devastated parts of Japan. Aflac happens to be the largest insurance company in Japan; needless to say, Gottfried was fired.[79]

Rosanne Barr was removed from her own show because she made a racist comment on Twitter about Valerie Jarett.[80] Kathy Griffin was cut off from endorsements and entertainment opportunities when she held up a fake severed head of then President Trump and posted the picture to Twitter.[81]

Those are just a few examples. Numerous people have suddenly found themselves unemployable in the past few years after things they'd foolishly posted or tweeted in the past came back to haunt them in the present. And while I find cancel culture repugnant in every way, since we have all said or done stupid things throughout our lives, the best defense against this offense is to never record certain kinds of thoughts publicly.

We have an unlimited opportunity to share our thoughts online. What gets shared the most? The dirt. The gossip. The nasty comments. The rants. Solomon has three words for you when the opportunity to unleash your fury arises: don't do it.

I speak from experience. One of my earliest lessons in the workplace involved a very difficult shift manager who loved to swear at the employees and belittle them. I had a hard time with this, so after my shift manager swore at me once, I decided to write my manager an email. Well, my manager took the email to the head boss's office. I'll give you one guess about which of the two of us was in hot water that afternoon—and it wasn't the shift manager.

I've had similar experiences as the head pastor of Waters Church. I've written down things that shouldn't have been written, and they got back to the person I wrote them about. The aftermath wasn't pretty. I've had people reach out to me, hoping to draw me into conversations about someone they were hoping to dig up some dirt on. I've learned to walk away from those situations without giving them what they're looking for.

Your words have power. They can be used for good, or they can be used for ill (Ephesians 4:29). It's up to you to learn how to use them wisely. When the wolves Jesus talked about receive words of blessing, they see them as words of cursing. They aren't getting the reaction they want, so they run away.

When dealing with difficult people who are intentionally or unconsciously making life difficult for you, look for the good things in their character and speak blessings into their life that elevate those good traits. I'm not telling you to butter them up. I'm telling you to look for the good.

When you actively look for the good in people who persecute or annoy you, it doesn't just change how you perceive them. It can change how they perceive themselves, and it can change how they perceive you.

CHRIST FACED DIFFICULT PEOPLE FOR YOU

He himself bore our sins in his body on the tree, that we might die to
sin and live to righteousness. By his wounds you have been healed.
—1 PETER 2:24 (ESV)

Let Christ lead you through the difficult relationships in your
life by remembering He faced difficult people for you. He faced
Pilate, who washed his hands and wouldn't stand up for Jesus. He
faced the chief priests and religious leaders who were jealous and
envious of His ministry. He faced the Roman centurions who tor-
tured Him before stretching Him out on a cross and nailing spikes
through His wrists and through His feet.

He faced all those people. For you.

The gospel addresses how we respond to difficult people: when
someone is bothering you, remember you were once bothersome
to God and He loved you through it. In 1 Peter 2:13 and 2:15
(ESV), Peter writes, "Be subject *for the Lord's sake* to every human
institution.... For this is the will of God, that by doing good you
should put to silence the ignorance of foolish people" (emphasis
mine).

In verse 18 (ESV), Peter says, "Servants, be subject to your masters with all respect, not only to the good and gentle but also to
the unjust." Show respect to your bosses, your teachers, and your
supervisors. Not just the good ones, but also the bad ones.

And then in 1 Peter 3:1 (ESV), he states, "Likewise, wives, be
subject to your own husbands, so that even if some do not obey
the word, they may be won without a word by the conduct of their
wives." Ladies, if your husband isn't following God's command to
love you the way Christ loved the church, love him anyway and
show him respect *for your own sake*. Instead of poking and prod-

ding at him, show him Christ's love. That behavior will win him back over to the Lord.

These are very hard choices we are to make. But Peter gives us the impetus for this: "For to this you have been called, because Christ also suffered for you, leaving you an example, so that you might follow in his steps" (1 Peter 2:21 ESV).

"*Suffered for you.*" Underline those words in your Bible. Write them down and hang them on the bathroom mirror. Jesus suffered living with difficult people *for you.*

Peter goes on to say in verses 23–24 (ESV), "When he was reviled, he did not revile in return; when he suffered, he did not threaten, but continued entrusting himself to him who judges justly. He himself bore our sins in his body on the tree, that we might die to sin and live to righteousness. By his wounds you have been healed."

In other words, Jesus faced the hostility of difficult people who hated him and berated Him, and His response was silent and confident trust in the Father's plan—all because of His love for you. And when you are looking to Him to be your ultimate source of fulfillment—rather than to others—you can give difficult people the same grace and patience God extends to you.

GOD HAS A PURPOSE FOR THE DIFFICULT PEOPLE IN YOUR LIFE

God can and will use that difficult person in your life to make you a better person for life. That's the whole purpose for God's University class in difficult people, and God has seen purpose to put you in that class for such a time as this. That person might rub you the wrong way but could also be *sharpening* you. That person might wear on your last nerve but could be forcing you to be less concerned about what you *feel.* That person might lie about you or try to deceive you but could be helping you find new appreciation for the truth.

NEVER FORGET: *YOU* ARE DIFFICULT

You know I had to get to this point. How easy it is to see life as if we are the starring cast member of a cosmic television show. Again, some of us need a personal Copernican revolution to remember we are not the center of the universe. So while we will struggle with difficult people, the humbling reality is to note that we are difficult as well. There are parts of our personality, or certain entrenched, sinful habits, that hurt others and bring pain to those around us. John reminds us of this invaluable truth: "If we say we have no sin, we deceive ourselves, and the truth is not in us" (1 John 1:8 ESV). Yes, hard as it is to imagine, we ourselves need work to become a better version of ourselves.

Now the good news: Jesus loves us through it all. He faced difficult people to bring you home. And He stands by us through each difficult moment we create. Nothing separates us from His love. So with Him walking with us, changing and transforming us, we can both learn from the difficult people in our lives and become less difficult people in the lives of others.

The gospel's answer to dealing with difficult people is realizing that you were the object of difficult conditions for Christ, and now you're His healed representative of reconciliation for others.

WORKBOOK

||||||||||||||||||||||||||||||||||||

Chapter Six Questions

Question: How do you tend to react to the difficult people in your life? Do these reactions represent the kind of person you want to be? How do you react when other people reveal that they find you difficult? What lessons can you learn both from interacting with difficult people and from the realization that some people find you difficult?

_____

_____

_____

_____

_____

_____

_____

_____

_____

_____

_____

Question: Are there any difficult people in your life right now? In what specific ways can you see God using them to develop you? Are there any areas in which you need to intentionally pursue growth through this difficult relationship? If so, what are those areas, and what steps can you take to start growing in those areas?

_____

_____

_____

_____

_____

_____

_____

_____

_____

_____

_____

_____

Journal: Write a prayer expressing your gratitude to Jesus for facing difficult people for you and showing you a better way. Express the areas you know you need to grow in, and invite God to do a work in your heart and give you His perspective and His character.

_____

_____

_____

_____

_____

_____

_____

_____

_____

_____

_____

Action: "Jesus suffered for you." Use this phrase as a reminder of all Christ endured on your behalf, and allow it to encourage you with the endurance and patience you need to face the difficulties in your life. If you find it helpful, post it somewhere you will regularly see it.

_____

_____

_____

_____

_____

_____

_____

_____

_____

_____

_____

Chapter Six Notes

|||||||||||||||||||||||||||||||||||||||||||||||||||||||||||

Life: Exhausting or Exhilarating?

The end of the matter; all has been heard. Fear God and keep his commandments, for this is the whole duty of man. For God will bring every deed into judgment, with every secret thing, whether good or evil.
—ECCLESIASTES 12:13 (ESV)

hen we get to Ecclesiastes 11, we meet the third turn in the book. In the first six chapters, we see the result of Solomon's early years of chasing fame, fortune, power, and achievement—much like most of us Americans do during the first half of our lives. He didn't just chase it; he got it. But all this did was prove to him that he was still lacking something vital in his life. In the second part of the book, he shares what he learned from that experience and offers us wisdom to navigate life's challenges so that we never have to run on empty.

Here in the third and final part, Solomon brings us to the conclusion of our lives—the ultimate point, if you will, of existence. And that point is simple: *worship* the Lord.

Worship of the Lord is not just a good idea; worship is an expressed commandment in both the Old and New Testaments.

Worship of the Lord is what we are made for. And like a car engine that only succeeds in driving with the wheels forward, your life is designed to glorify God. Without participating in that ultimate goal, you will always feel some semblance of emptiness. Again, your "self" falls far short of being able to fulfill you. This is where worship comes in. Eugene Peterson said, "Worship is the strategy by which we interrupt our preoccupation with ourselves and attend to the presence of God."[82] You were made to focus your life on Someone eternally more important than you—and that's where emptiness finally ends.

If you'll permit me to use a sports analogy here, I like to think of these last two chapters as Solomon's "locker room speech." If you haven't heard a locker room speech in life, I'm sure you've seen at least one example in a movie or TV show, where the coach amps up his team before their big, final confrontation with their cross-town rival. The locker room speech is all about spurring the players on before they charge out onto the field and into victory.

HOW YOU VIEW LIFE WILL DETERMINE HOW YOU DO LIFE

How do you look at life? Do you realize that part of life is a fight? Maybe you feel like you get up in the morning anticipating great things only to come home at night feeling utterly defeated. If aren't paying attention to the fact that *life is a fight*, then you're not going to keep your guard up, which means you're going to get punched in the mouth or have your feet swiped out from beneath you.

There are so many wrong ways to view life and its troubles. Some people look at life like it's nothing but a great pain. So they run away from every potential problem rather than risking any chance of feeling discomfort, not realizing that sometimes the pain is good. Sometimes you need to be pricked a little bit in your spirit, in your flesh, or in your mind. No pain, no gain, I'm sure you've heard.

Some people think that life is misery, and they are miserable. Their defeatist attitude makes them a chore for others to be around, so they often find themselves cut off from those who would otherwise bring joy into their lives. I know we say misery loves company, but let's be honest, nobody wants to be the company.

If you view life as a game rather than a battle, you may make some bad choices that you'll highly regret at the end of your life. If life is a joke, you'll think that what you do today doesn't matter in the long run, but when the end comes, you'll be the one who's not laughing.

If you consider life to be unspiritual, meaning you're only focused on having as much fun as possible in this world (and possibly squeaking into the next one), you'll see no real need to focus on spiritual things or engage in spiritual works. You'll leave this world without ever making an impact.

If we view life rightly, we'll do life rightly. But if we view life wrongly, we'll do life wrongly. Solomon addresses four *wrong* ways to do life in these final two chapters, and he shows us what we should do to avoid the bad plays that threaten our victory.

Life Is an Opportunity—Invest in It

Cast your bread upon the waters, for you will find it after many days. Give a portion to seven, or even to eight, for you know not what disaster may happen on earth. If the clouds are full of rain, they empty themselves on the earth, and if a tree falls to the south or to the north, in the place where the tree falls, there it will lie. He who observes the wind will not sow, and he who regards the clouds will not reap. As you do not know the way the

spirit comes to the bones in the womb of a woman with child, so you do
not know the work of God who makes everything.
—ECCLESIASTES 11:1–5 (ESV)

You've got a chance to invest in your life. What are you doing right now that is going to pay dividends years from now? I've thought about this one point more than any other in this chapter, because I think this one could set you up so well.

Verse 11:1 says, "Cast your bread upon the waters, for you will find it after many days." In Solomon's day, all trade was done on the waters. Merchants traveled by ship with goods from one country to trade with another. They faced the risk of storms and dead calms, of sickness and shipwrecks, all in the hopes of trading one thing of value for another thing of even greater value.

Solomon and Jesus both made it a point to tell us to take our goods, our skills, our gifts, and our finances and put them to use. We're supposed to trade them for something that will be of even greater value down the road. Yes, it is a good thing for us to do this for long-term financial gain, but we need to also invest ourselves in things such as relationships and pursuits that are going to result in long-term growth over time, which will bring lasting joy to us into our old age.

Life is an opportunity for us to do things that matter. We properly invest in life when we attempt multiple ventures. So do different things. Try something that scares you. Change up your routine. Don't let what *may* happen keep you from doing something!

I went back to school at age thirty-five. At first I thought, "I'm too old for this. School is for kids." Silly rabbit. If you have breath in your lungs, God says you've got a day to take advantage of. You're not too old to attempt something new.

I look back on my life thus far and am most thankful for the things I tried despite how I thought they were going to turn out. The first time I preached, I stunk. I tried again. I stunk. I keep trying, and I'm still stinking on occasion; but people keep showing up, so I'm going to keep teaching.

I recently took up tennis, and I didn't start off stinking! I was actually pretty good my first time on the court. So I joined a league and I got trounced in my first two weeks. I actually apologized to the second guy who trounced me. His response? "Nonsense. You're out here trying."

Put yourself out there, my friend. Invest your life in something. And then keep investing. If you play life too safe, you're going to end up wondering why it's so boring. However, be aware that the moment you're about to try something new in life, all the negative voices will start lunging at you at the same time. And all the things that could possibly happen to wreck or upend your plans are going to flood your mind.

Side note—I would be remiss if I didn't end a discussion on investment and responsibility without saying this: the best investment you can make in life is in people. When Solomon says in Ecclesiastes 11:2, "Give a portion to seven, or even to eight," he is talking about investing in people. People are God's treasures. People are the only thing you can take with you to heaven. They are who Christ died for. And the work of bringing people into God's kingdom is the work He commissioned His disciples, and everyone who calls on the name of Christ, to do (Matthew 28:16–20).

Senator and astronaut John Glenn said, "If there's one thing I've learned in my years on this planet, it's that the happiest and most fulfilled people are those who devoted themselves to something bigger and more profound than merely their own self-interest." [83] I'll take that investment advice from a man who's (literally) been around the world. If you have a home church, get plugged into community groups and in-home Bible studies with people in different stages of life. Look for ways you can invest in building those relationships rather than just showing up, sharing a few tweet-worthy quips, and then leaving. Are there ministry opportunities in your community—both through your church and outside your church? Find one that can utilize your God-given interests and talents to build relationships and invest in the lives of people who might never set foot in a church.

People matter to God. Invest in them.

Life Is a Mystery—Trust God with It

> If the clouds are full of rain, they empty themselves on the earth, and if a tree falls to the south or to the north, in the place where the tree falls, there it will lie. He who observes the wind will not sow, and he who regards the clouds will not reap.
> —ECCLESIASTES 11:3–4 (ESV)

I love how the New Century Version translates verse 4: "Those who wait for perfect weather will never plant seeds; those who look at every cloud will never harvest crops." [84]

There are people in life who go out looking for problems. They need to be one hundred percent sure about something before they'll even consider taking the first step. If they aren't completely "at peace," they won't take the risk.

I've yet to take a risk that hasn't scared me to some degree. And there's never been a time in my life where everything around me is "at peace" or perfectly lined up to move ahead in trying something new. There can be obstacles, barriers, and plenty of distractions coming at me at once, yet I can still be at peace with God at the core of my being.

That peace is the only peace I need. Because if I have peace with God, then I know that I'm in the palm of His hand. I know that no matter what happens, He's going to work it out for my good, and no matter what the storm is like on the outside, the relationship I have with Him is solid. That risk I take can ultimately fail; I recognize this going into everything I do. But that doesn't scare me because the one thing I need to be sure of in life—my eternal standing in Christ—is secure. Everything else is a bonus.

If you are in Christ, the same is true for you.

Things are going to happen, Solomon says. Hard things. Scary things. Some of those things we can predict and prepare for (verse 3), but we can't plan for and predict everything (verse 4). My friend, if you keep worrying about the things you can't predict or control, you'll never do anything and you'll miss out on some of life's greatest experiences.

Perhaps you're reading this and thinking, "That's great, Tim. But I have no idea what I'm supposed to be doing right now. I don't even see a wisp of opportunity on the horizon." Solomon has advice for you, too. In verses 5 and 6, he says:

> As you do not know the way the spirit comes to the bones in the womb
> of a woman with child, so you do not know the work of God who makes
> everything. In the morning sow your seed, and at evening withhold
> not your hand, for you do not know which will prosper, this or that, or
> whether both alike will be good.

Now, Solomon uses agricultural principles here, but they can be translated into modern times: Commit to today's responsibilities. Finish what you started. You don't know how your business or industry is going to go in the future, so guess what you do today? You work hard at it.

This is a personal text for me. When I first sat down to begin working on this study in early 2019, my daughter was eighteen and making plans about going to college. She had all these questions about what school she should go to, what field of study she should pursue, and how she was going to pay for tuition. But there was one possibility that never crossed her mind: what happens when a massive pandemic begins sweeping the globe at the end of 2019, effectively shutting down the world in early 2020? Her graduation from high school was nothing like I imagined it would be: an empty corridor with just our family, her, and two administrators. No band, no crowd, no grand presentation. Though there are no perfection conditions, I felt so bad she did not have that experience.

Not one of us could have planned for the far-reaching effects of a microscopic virus, yet it happened all the same. And it's affected us all in different ways. As I work on this book in mid-2022, most of us are still trying to figure out how to move forward. My daughter is still wrestling between school choices. My second-born has graduated high school, and my third child, who has just turned ten, believes he's smarter than my wife and me. You cannot wait for perfect conditions, but you can let the lack of perfect conditions stall your life. The choice is yours.

Solomon's advice for us is simple. Show up. Do the work that's right in front of you. And leave the future to God.

Life Is an Adventure—Enjoy It

Light is sweet, and it is pleasant for the eyes to see the sun. So if a person lives many years, let him rejoice in them all; but let him

remember that the days of darkness will be many. All that comes is
vanity. Rejoice, O young man, in your youth, and let your heart cheer
you in the days of your youth... Remove vexation from your heart, and
put away pain from your body, for youth and the dawn of life are vanity.
—ECCLESIASTES 11:7–9A, 11:10 (ESV)

Do you enjoy your life? Do you ever stop and think that joy in life is commanded, not suggested, in Scripture? Philippians 4:4 says, "Rejoice in the Lord always; again I will say, rejoice" (ESV). And here in Ecclesiastes 11:8 and 9, it effectively says to rejoice, but rejoice responsibly.

Scripture tells us to enjoy the good things because bad things will inevitably happen. If we don't rejoice in the good times, we won't have anything to carry us through the bad times. Troubles are a part of the human adventure. If we fixate on them, they're going to completely warp how we view life and the people living alongside us. We're going to look for the bad, and we're going to find it. But when viewed from a joyful context, bad things also serve a useful purpose. They help us remember the good times.

Mark Twain said, "What is joy without sorrow? What is success without failure? What is a win without a loss? What is health without illness? You have to experience each if you are to appreciate the other." [85]

Two tasks are given to us in verse 10 to help us enjoy life more:

1. First, remove vexation (anger, grief, irritation, unforgiveness) from your heart. Are you focusing your thoughts and meditations on what is hurtful and painful to you? Are you holding onto something that someone did to you twenty years ago, five years ago, or even a few days ago that is still making you shake with anger? You have to break out of it.

Depending on the situation, you may need to talk to someone. Get a friend you can confide in. Find a godly counselor who can come alongside you. We who are in Christ have been called into a spirit of forgiveness. This is to be an active, present, and constant part of our lives. Christians don't just think about forgiveness or wait for the person who wronged us to apologize. We forgive now. We see this in the Lord's prayer when we say, "Forgive us our debts as we also have forgiven those who owe us debts."

Forgiveness isn't forgetting and acting like nothing happened; it's casting off and letting go of something that holds us in misery and pain. It's turning our hurts over to God and trusting that He will make them right in His perfect time.

2. *Secondly, verse 10 tells us to put away pain from your body.* (Please note the order of these two statements: first deal with the inside, then address what's outside.) Stop ignoring the signals from your brain that are telling you something is wrong with your body. If you're in physical pain, seek out the cause and do something about it. This may mean taking a few aspirin to get rid of a headache so you can focus your kids. It might mean making an appointment with your doctor to address an on-going health issue that isn't resolving itself. It might mean focusing on moving around more, getting more exercise, or changing your diet. You only have one body in this lifetime. Take care of it.

Life Is a Breath—Maximize It

> Remember also your Creator in the days of your youth, before the evil days come and the years draw near of which you will say, "I have no pleasure in them"; before the sun and the light and the moon and the stars are darkened and the clouds return after the rain.
>
> —ECCLESIASTES 12:1 (ESV)

As a pastor, one of the hardest things I'm called to do is officiate funerals for young people. One of the best serve-team members at my church came down with COVID-19 in late 2021. The church prayed and prayed, and he got worse and worse. Eventually, I preached at his funeral, with his parents in the front row. Life is not supposed to be like that. But that day reminded me that all lives end, and no one knows when. Do not let it pass you by!

In chapter 12, Solomon teaches us that old age is not guaranteed for anyone, so we need to maximize today. Enjoy the gifts you've been given, serve the Lord with a spirit of gladness, and make the most of the opportunities (both the good and the difficult) that are in front of you.

Solomon speaks poetically of the aging body in verse 3 when he says: "…in the day when the keepers of the house tremble, and the strong men are bent, and the grinders cease because they are few, and those who look through the windows are dimmed" (ESV). He uses metaphors to describe shaking hands ("keepers of the house"), bent legs ("strong men"), worn down teeth ("grinders"), and failing eyesight ("windows").

In verse 4, he goes on with his description, saying, "And the doors on the street are shut—when the sound of the grinding is low, and one rises up at the sound of a bird, and all the daughters of song are brought low" (ESV), describing the loss of hearing, the loss of energy, and the loss of sleep.

Ecclesiastes 12:5 (ESV) reads, "They are afraid also of what is high, and terrors are in the way; the almond tree blossoms, the grasshopper drags itself along, and desire fails, because man is going to his eternal home, and the mourners go about the streets." When an almond tree blooms, its blossoms are a grayish color, which Solomon uses to describe the graying of hair. And grasshoppers that used to jump with excitement at every little thing now struggle to move at all. Perhaps you're reaching a point where you're beginning to relate.

Finally, he says, "desire fails." I'll leave that one to your imagination. Let's just say they didn't have a pill for that ailment in Solomon's day.

Solomon ends his cheerful poem by saying a final day is coming, whether you're ready or not, when your body will "return to the dust it was" and your spirit will return "to the God who gave it," (Ecclesiastes 12:7 ESV). But before "the silver cord is snapped, or the golden bowl is broken" (Ecclesiastes 12:6 ESV), you must be ready. Think of these things before they happen.

Why? So you can use your youth to create a life that flourishes with joy, contentment, and meaning.

Life Is a Stewardship—Surrender It

The end of the matter; all has been heard. Fear God and keep his commandments, for this is the whole duty of man. For God will bring every deed into judgment, with every secret thing, whether good or evil.
—ECCLESIASTES 12:13–14 (ESV)

These last two verses mark the end of Solomon's locker room speech to us. And he sums it all up by saying that your life is really not yours; it's a gift. Remember your Creator (verse 1) and that God has created you to do life a certain way. That's why He gave us His word in the form of the Bible—so that we could learn how to do life the way we were created to do life.

That's what wisdom is. It helps you make better decisions today so that you have fewer regrets tomorrow. Here's where our country gets it so wrong every single day: the Democrats tell you, "It's your body," and the Republicans tell you, "It's your money," but

God tells you, "It's all Mine. Your body is Mine. Your thoughts are Mine. Your heart is Mine. And all you have been given is Mine." If you want to live well, you will live with that in mind and you won't side with the people who tell you otherwise. Instead, tell God, "I surrender. I give You my life."

God is the eternal judge, to whom we'll all give a final account whether our deeds were good or evil. We tend to think the judgment of God is a bad thing—and I get that. But I also want to make one thing clear: if *God* is not your judge, *someone else* is. And you make them your judge the day you start doing things either to win their approval or out of fear of what they might think if you don't go along with them.

Are they worth it?

The end of Ernest Hemingway's life, as detailed by his many biographers, was fraught with paranoia, anxiety, and depression; he had an ailing body and a confused mind. This great outdoorsman of the twentieth century chased the applause, acclaim, and accomplishments of a celebrity author, and he got them all! But what of his end? His lust for adventure led to accidents that damaged him physically and mentally. His quest for professional respect left him anxious that he had lost his abilities as a writer. His jumps from one lover to another doubtless left him scarred. His life was both extraordinary and deeply sad. He's heralded for its highlights, but his story serves as a warning for us today to "fear God and keep His commandments, for this is the whole duty of man" (Ecclesiastes 12:13).

If God is not your judge, then the members of your political party, or your political opponents, are. If God is not your judge, then your boss will be, your spouse will be, or your friends will be. The list goes on. You may give them that power over you now, but in the end, you are not ultimately accountable to them. But if you live with God as your judge, I guarantee you will make the decisions He wants you to make. And you will be so much happier and fulfilled! Because at the end of all things, His opinion is the only one that counts, and He knows a life spent honoring Him will bring you the deepest satisfaction.

In the end, He is the One whose love for you is eternal.

WORKBOOK

||||||||||||||||||||||||||||||||||||||

Chapter Seven Questions

Question: What is your view of life? What are you expecting to get out of life? In what ways is your view oversaturated with an unrealistic ideal? In what ways is your view overly pessimistic? How can you have a more balanced view of—and therefore approach to—life?

_____

_____

_____

_____

_____

_____

_____

_____

_____

_____

_____

Question: What aspect of life (an opportunity, a mystery, an adventure, a breath, a stewardship) do you find the easiest to embrace? Which do you find the most difficult to embrace? What changes can you make in your perspective to embrace all the aspects of life more readily?

_____

_____

_____

_____

_____

_____

_____

_____

_____

_____

_____

_____

Journal: What do you feel when you think about life being but a breath—here today and gone tomorrow? How would you spend your days if the reality of the shortness of life truly sunk in? If you knew you only had a certain number of days, how would you use them? What would you do? Does this reflection reveal any changes you need to make to the way you are spending your time currently?

_____

_____

_____

_____

_____

_____

_____

_____

_____

_____

_____

Action: Have you truly surrendered your life to God? Spend some time in prayer asking God to show you what it means for you to give your life to Him. Ask Him to fill you with the willingness to trust Him with it all. And ask Him to reveal to you if there are any ways you are withholding from Him, as well as what changes you need to make to demonstrate that all you have belongs to Him.

Chapter Seven Notes

||||||||||||||||||||||||||||||||||||||||||||

A Life That's Full

have one final question for you before we close this book. If how
you view life determines how you do life, how is your life doing?
Maybe it's time for you to decide to come to Christ. Maybe
it's time for you to decide to get involved in your local church.
Maybe it's time for you to decide to try that new venture in life
and get involved in some new thing—to put your hand to something you've never given yourself to before. Or maybe it's just time
for you to enjoy today.

This is why we do what we do: because we believe that the God
who is above all things has created us to live a life that is abun-
dantly full *in Him*. And so, we say goodbye to Ecclesiastes considering how God blesses us in this life with glimpses of heaven.

Once, a woman in our church chose to get more involved and
start a small group. Though she wasn't sure at first that she could
do it, she would prove to be an able and effective small group
leader. As part of her preparation to begin the group, we asked her
to do something many people find uncomfortable: post an invi-
tation to the group on social media. She posted a video in which
she talked about the small group and shared a little about herself.

Elsewhere, the next day, a man was telling his mechanic, "I just want to see my daughter once before I die."

The mechanic asked her name and searched for her on social media. He showed the man the woman's small group video and asked, "Is that your daughter?"

And the man answered, "That's my daughter! I know that's my daughter!"

This small group leader had been attending our church for five years. She hadn't seen her father since she was seven. Forty-two years after she had last seen him, he called her at work, and they reconnected. It was something she had thought would never happen.

But God makes things happen, and this woman is now filled with gratitude that He brought her dad back into her life. She got a little taste of heaven.

We don't need to fear or avoid what life might bring our way. When our life is in the hands of the One who made it, we are empowered to embrace and enjoy it.

About the Author

Tim Hatch is the pastor of Waters Church, a multi-site and international congregation originating in New England, and the host of *TimHatchLive* on YouTube, where he teaches through Scripture verse by verse and addresses social issues from a Christian viewpoint. He is married to Cheryl, and together they have three children—Alivia, Connor, and Jake. Tim earned his master's in theology from Knox Theological Seminary in 2015. His passion is for the Church to live up to her calling in this generation, seeking to share the gospel and pass on gospel-centered leadership to future generations.

Endnotes

||||||||||||||||||||||||||||

1   Putnam, Thomas. "Hemingway on War and Its Aftermath." *Prologue Magazine* 38, no. 1 (Spring 2006). National Archives. https://www.archives.gov/publications/prologue/2006/spring/hemingway.html.

2   Pak, Eudie. "The Many Wives of Ernest Hemingway." Biography. April 6, 2021. https://www.biography.com/news/ernest-hemingway-wives.

3   Putnam, "Hemingway on War and Its Aftermath."

4   Hemingway, Ernest. *A Farewell to Arms*. Scribner, 1929.

5   Jones, S. E., K. A. Ethier, M. Hertz, et al. "Mental Health, Suicidality, and Connectedness Among High School Students During the COVID-19 Pandemic—Adolescent Behaviors and Experiences Survey, United States, January–June 2021." *Morbidity and Mortality Weekly Report Supplements* 71, no. 3 (2022): p. 16–21. DOI: http://dx.doi.org/10.15585/mmwr.su7103a3.

6   White, Aaron M., I-Jen P. Castle, Patricia A. Powell, et al. "Alcohol-Related Deaths During the COVID-19 Pandemic." *Journal of the American Medical Association* 327, no. 17 (2022): p. 1704–1706. doi:10.1001/jama.2022.4308.

7   Hill, Catey. "The Dark Reasons So Many Rich People Are Miserable Human Beings." MarketWatch. February 22, 2018. https://www. marketwatch.com/story/the-dark-reasons-so-

many-rich-people-are-miserable-human-beings-2018-02-22.

8   Sifferlin, Alexandra. "Here's How Happy Americans Are Right Now." *Time.* July 26, 2017. https://time.com/4871720P/how-happy-are-americans/.

9   Helliwell, John, Richard Layard, Jeffrey D. Sachs, Jan-Emmanuel De Neve, Lara Aknin, and Shun Wang. *World Happiness Report.* Edited by Sharon Paculor. 2021. https://happiness-report.s3.amazonaws.com/2021/WHR+21.pdf.

10 Drillinger, Meagan. "Depression Symptoms 3 Times Higher During COVID-19 Lockdown." Healthline. https://www.healthline.com/health-news/depression-symptoms-3-times-higher-during-covid-19-lockdown.

11 Edwards, Erika. "Emergency Room Doctors Beg for Help Treating Children with Mental Health Illnesses." NBC News. 16 August 2023. https://www.nbcnews.com/health/health-news/emergency-room-doctors-beg-help-treating-children-mental-health-illnes-rc-na99951.

12 Pfeiffer, Robert H. "Assyria and Israel." *Rivista Degli Studi Orientali* 32 (1957): p. 145–54. http://www.jstor.org/stable/41922829.

13 Kwapis, Ken, dir. *The Office.* "Finale." Season 9, episodes 24–25. Aired May 16, 2013, on NBC.

14 StudyLight.org, "Strong's #1892 – לְבָה." https://www.studylight.org/lexicons/eng/hebrew/1892.html.

15 Dearborn, Mary V. *Ernest Hemingway: A Biography.* Kindle edition. Knopf Doubleday, 2017, p. 234–235.

16 Americans Library, "James Monroe." https://www.americaslibrary. gov/aa/monroe/aa_monroe_subj.html.

17 Hemingway, Ernest. *Men at War.* Bramhall House, 1942.

18 Fleiss, Mike. *The Bachelor.* Warner Bros. Television Distribution, 2002–present.

19 Hearn, Patrick. "The Amazon Echo Loop Is a Smart Ring That Puts Alexa at Your Fingertips." Digitaltrends. September 25, 2019. https:// www.digitaltrends.com/wearables/amazon-echo-loop-smart-ring-alexa-features-price-specs-release-date/.

20 Patterson, Ben. "Amazon Unveils Next-Gen Echo Frames, but Stops Selling the Echo Loop Smart Ring." TechHive. November 19, 2020. https://www.techhive.com/article/3597991/amazon-unveils-next-gen-echo-frames-drops-echo-loop-smart-ring.html.

21 Ravenscraft, Eric. "What Is the Metaverse, Exactly?" Wired. November 25, 2021. https://www.wired.com/story/what-is-the-metaverse/.

22 Calvin, John. Institutes of the Christian Religion. 1536. Presbyterian Publishing Corporation, 1960, p. 108.

23 Enhanced Strong's Lexicon, "tetelestai." By James Strong. Woodside Bible Fellowship, 1995.

24 The Byrds. "Turn! Turn! Turn!" Lyrics by Pete Seeger. "Turn! Turn! Turn!" Columbia Records, 1965.

25 Billboard. "The Hot 100: Week of December 4, 1965." https:// www.billboard.com/charts/hot-100/1965-12-04/.

26 Hinchee, Lawrence Edward. "This Song Comes from the Bible." Beat. https://vocal.media/beat/this-song-comes-from-the-bible.

27 Tillman, Nola Taylor. "Nicolaus Copernicus Biography: Facts and Discoveries." Space.com. January 17, 2022. https://www.space.com/15684-nicolaus-copernicus.html.

28 Blue Letter Bible, "Strong's H2263 – ḥāḇaq." https://www.blueletterbible.org/lexicon/h2263/kjv/wlc/0-1/.

29 Unicef. "A Child Under 15 Dies Every Five Seconds Around the World—UN Report." September 17, 2018. https://www.unicef.org/press-releases/child-under-15-dies-every-five-

seconds-around-world-un-report.

30 "Bourdain Off the Cuff: Vietnam." *Anthony Bourdain Parts Unknown.* https://explorepartsunknown.com/vietnam/ bourdain-off-the-cuff-vietnam/.

31 Curtis, Lucas. "How Long Would It Take Voyager 1 to Reach Alpha Centauri?" Quora answer. 2021. https://www.quora. com/How-long-would-it-take-Voyager-1-to-reach-Alpha-Centauri.

32 *The New York Times.* "At Coachella, The Gospel According to Kanye West." April 21, 2019. https://www.nytimes. com/2019/04/21/arts/music/kanye-west-coachella.html.

33 Wax, Trevin. "Kanye West, Justin Bieber, and What to Make of Celebrity Conversions." The Gospel Coalition. September 23, 2019. https://www.thegospelcoalition.org/blogs/trevin-wax/kanye-west-justin-bieber-make-celebrity-conversions/.

34 Baron, Zach. "Brad Pitt Is Still Searching." GQ. September 16, 2019. https://www.gq.com/story/brad-pitt-cover-profile-october-2019.

35 White, Lisa Beth. "Carmichael, Amy Beatrice (1867–1951)." History of Missiology. https://www.bu.edu/ missiology/missionary-biography/c-d/carmichael-amy-beatrice-1867-1951/.

36 Allyn, Bobby. "Amber Guyger, Ex-Officer Who Killed Man in His Apartment, Given 10 Years in Prison." NPR. October 2, 2019. https:// www.npr.org/2019/10/02/766454839/amber-guyger-ex-officer-who-killed-man-in-his-apartment-given-10-years-in-prison.

37 Allyn, "Amber Guyger."

38 MSN. "30 Surprising Facts About How We Spend Our Time." April 5, 2015. https://www.msn.com/en-gb/lifestyle/life/30-surprising-facts-about-how-we-spend-our-time/ss-BBjeV3f.

39 *The Atlantic.* "Attention, Employers: Millennials Have Made Their Demands." https://www.theatlantic.com/sponsored/allstate/attention-employers-millennials-have-made-their-demands/219/.

40 Ratner, Brett. *The Family Man.* Universal Pictures, December 22, 2000.

41 Fuller, Simon. *American Idol.* American Broadcasting Company, 2002–present.

42 Leonhardt, Megan. "Here's the Net Worth Americans Say You need To Be Considered Wealthy." CNBC. May 12, 2021. https://www.cnbc.com/2021/05/12/net-worth-to-be-considered-wealthy-in-2021.html?utm_term=Autofeed&utm_medium=Social&utm_content=Main&utm_source=Twitter#Echobox=1620821471.

43 *The Tonight Show Starring Johnny Carson.* National Broadcasting Company, 1962–1992.

44 Assemblies of God Heritage. "Evangelist Charles S. Price." 2008, p.3. https://ifphc.org/-/media/FPHC/Heritage-Magazine/2008.pdf.

45 Global Teen Challenge. "Global Locations." https://www.globaltc. org/global-locations/.

46 Monticello. "Knowledge Is Power (Quotation)." https://www.monticello.org/site/research-and-collections/knowledge-power-quotation#_note-0.

47 Got Questions. "Is It Possible to Be So Heavenly Minded That You Are of No Earthly Good?

48 Constable, Thomas L. *The Bible Knowledge Commentary: An Exposition of the Scriptures.* Vol. 1. Victor Books, 1985, p. 522.

49 Unger, Merrill F. *The New Unger's Bible Dictionary.* Moody Press, 1988.

50 Fratti, Karen. "Why We're Worried About Aaron Carter's

Baby." Nicki Swift. April 22, 2020. https://www.nickiswift. com/203702/why-were-worried-about-aaron-carters-baby/.

51   AP News. "Aaron Carter Was 'So Scared' When He Dropped 115 Pounds." https://apnews.com/article/ bc035511855e4cb392039e50faaa9694.

52   Basu, Arunima. "Aaron Carter Used to Be Worth Millions … Here's What His Net Worth Is Now." TheThings. May 9, 2020. https://www.thethings.com/aaron-carter-used-to-be-worth-millions-heres-what-his-net-worth-is-now/.

53   Melas, Chloe, and Emma Tucker. "Aaron Carter, Singer, Dead at 34." CNN. November 6, 2022. https://www.cnn.com/2022/11/05/ entertainment/aaron-carter-obit/index.html.

54   The Royal Society for Public Health. "#Status of Mind." https:// www.rsph.org.uk/about-us/news/instagram-ranked-worst-for-young-people-s-mental-health.html.

55   Romo, Vanessa. "Whistleblower's Testimony Has Resurfaced Facebook's Instagram Problem." NPR. October 5, 2021. https://www. npr.org/2021/10/05/1043194385/ whistleblowers-testimony-facebook-instagram.

56   Lady Gaga. Born This Way. Streamline, May 23, 2011.

57   Kempis, Thomas. The Imitation of Christ. CreateSpace Independent Publishing Platform, 2015.

58   Galli, Mark, and Ted Olsen. 131 Christians Everyone Should Know. Broadman and Holman Publishers, 2000, p. 89.

59   Kiecolt-Glaser, Janice K., et al. "Close Relationships, Inflammation, and Health." Neuroscience and Biobehavioral Reviews 35, no. 1 (September 2010). doi:10.1016/j. neubiorev.2009.09.003. https://www. ncbi.nlm.nih.gov/ pmc/articles/PMC2891342/.

60   Wiersbe, Warren W. Be Satisfied. Victor Books, 1996, p. 86.

61   Lady Gage. "Applause." Track no. 15 on Artpop. Interscope,

2013.

62 Moukarbel, Chris, dir. *Gaga: Five Foot Two.* Netflix, 2017.

63 Blue Letter Bible, "Strong's H6233 – ʿōšeq." https://www.blueletterbible.org/lexicon/h6233/kjv/wlc/0-1/.

64 Nelson, Thomas. *Wiersbe Study Bible, Red Letter: Be Transformed by the Power of God's Word.* Thomas Nelson, 2019, p.965.

65 Lewis, Clive Staples. *The Problem of Pain.* HarperOne, 2001.

66 Swanson, James. *Dictionary of Biblical Languages with Semantic Domains: Hebrew (Old Testament).* Logos Research Systems, Inc., 1997.

67 Welsh, Kristy. "How Mental Health Affects Physical Health." LiveScience. October 4, 2021. https://www.livescience.com/how-mental-health-affects-physical-health.

68 Rey, Ariel R. "Report: Christians Live Healthier, Longer." The Christian Post. https://www.christianpost.com/news/report-christians-live-healthier-longer.html.

69 Ducharme, Jamie. "You Asked: Do Religious People Live Longer?" Time. February 15, 2018. https://time.com/5159848/do-religious-people-live-longer/.

70 Parisot, Dean. *Fun with Dick and Jane.* Sony Pictures Releasing. December 21, 2005.

71 History.com Editors. "George Floyd Is Killed by a Police Officer, Igniting Historic Protest." History. https://www.history.com/this-day-in-history/george-floyd-killed-by-police-officer.

72 Dienst, Jonathan, and Miles Miller. "Second NYPD Officer Dies After Friday Shooting in Harlem." NBC New York. January 26, 2022. https://www.nbcnewyork.com/news/local/2nd-nypd-officer-dies-after-friday-shooting-in-harlem/3513604/.

73 Wise, Robert. *The Sound of Music.* Twentieth Century Fox,

April 1, 1965.

74 Andrews, Julie, and Bill Lee. "Something Good." By Richard Rodgers. On *The Sound of Music* soundtrack. RCA, 1965.

75 Warrick, Joby. "Abu Bakr al-Baghdadi, Extremist Leader of Islamic State, Died at 48." Washington Post. https://www.washingtonpost.com/local/obituaries/abu-bakr-al-baghdadi-islamic-states-terrorist-in-chief-dies-at-48/2019/10/27/0d004abc-663d-11e7-8eb5-cbccc2e7bfbf_story.html.

76 Gladwell, Malcolm. *Outliers: The Story of Success*. Books Limited, 2008.

77 Luscombe, Belinda. "A Guy Read 50 Years Worth of Relationship Studies. He Came Up with 17 Strategies." Time. September 6, 2017. https://time.com/4927173/relationships-strategies-studies/.

78 Gottlieb, Lori. "What Brand Is Your Therapist?" *The New York Times*. November 23, 2012. https://www.nytimes.com/2012/11/25/magazine/psychotherapys-image-problem-pushes-some-therapists-to-become-brands.html.

79 Huffpost. "Gilbert Gottfried Fired As Aflac Duck After Japanese Tsunami Tweets." March 14, 2011. https://www.huffpost.com/entry/gilbert-gottfried-fired-aflac_n_835692.

80 *The New York Times*. "After Racist Tweet, Roseanne Barr's Show Is Canceled by ABC." May 9, 2018. https://www.nytimes.com/2018/05/29/business/media/roseanne-barr-offensive-tweets.html.

81 Kazin, Matthew. "Kathy Griffin Losing Sponsorship, Gifs After Gory Trump Photo." Fox Business. May 31, 2017. https://www.foxbusiness. com/features/kathy-griffin-losing-sponsorship-gigs-after-gory-trump-photo.

82 Peterson, Eugene. *A Long Obedience in the Same Direction*.

InterVarsity, 1980.

83 *Congressional Record: Proceedings and Debates of the ... Congress.* U.S. Government Printing Office, 2011, p. 11292.

84 Scripture taken from the New Century Version®. Copyright © 2005 by Thomas Nelson. Used by permission. All rights reserved.

85 Coenn, Daniel. *Mark Twain: His Words.* BookRix, 2014.

A free ebook edition is available with the purchase of this book.

To claim your free ebook edition:

1. Visit MorganJamesBOGO.com
2. Sign your name CLEARLY in the space
3. Complete the form and submit a photo of the entire copyright page
4. You or your friend can download the ebook to your preferred device

Morgan James BOGO™

A **FREE** ebook edition is available for you or a friend with the purchase of this print book.

CLEARLY SIGN YOUR NAME ABOVE

Instructions to claim your free ebook edition:
1. Visit MorganJamesBOGO.com
2. Sign your name CLEARLY in the space above
3. Complete the form and submit a photo of this entire page
4. You or your friend can download the ebook to your preferred device

Print & Digital Together Forever.

Snap a photo

Free ebook

Read anywhere

Printed in the USA
CPSIA information can be obtained
at www.ICGtesting.com
JSHW082239070624
64478JS00004B/6